CREATED
FOR
GOOD DEEDS

Mike O'Neal

21st CENTURY CHRISTIAN PUBLISHING

ISBN: 978-0-89098-917-3

Unless otherwise noted Scripture quotations are from the New American Standard Bible.

Scripture taken from the NEW AMERICAN STANDARD BIBLE®,

Copyright © 1960,1962,1963,1968,1971,1972,1973,1975,1977,1995 by The Lockman Foundation. Used by permission.

Cover design by Jonathan Edelhuber

Table of Contents

Preface & Acknowledgements

A couple of years ago, I had a heartrending discussion with one of the elders at my church regarding the life and death struggle he was undergoing with cancer, the details of which are in chapter 1. Because of a comment he made, I surprisingly walked away from that conversation contemplating the goodness of God. While thinking about this, I recalled that Paul used the word *good* several times in his letter to Titus, but I did not remember its use or context. So I opened my Bible to Titus and read it through several times in a row. Afterward, I came to believe that Paul's epistle to Titus was an exposition on *good deeds*, and Paul earnestly desired for the churches in Crete to thrive in this core aspect of Christian life.

I then started researching the topic of good deeds. Just shortly after I began this new thrust, Vic Pruitt, the pulpit minister at the Holly Hill Church of Christ in Florida, asked me to present a lesson in their summer series on the subject of equipping. God appeared to be at work, so I volunteered to provide a lesson titled "Equipping for Good Deeds." While preparing this class, a passion for the topic took hold of me. I knew that performing good deeds was to be a part of our daily walk, but I never understood how integral they were to God's plan for us. The phrase "good deeds" started jumping off the pages of my Bible in, what I believed to be, many of the cornerstone passages of the Christian faith.

The lesson I prepared for the Holly Hill Church of Christ became the groundwork for this book. Not only do I believe that you will find the technical content eye-opening and challenging, you will enjoy the many good deed stories in the book. At the end of each chapter you will find a section called "Good Deeds to Ponder." In each of these sections, you will find two real-life good deed stories gleaned from personal interviews, except one which contains an article used by permission from the Mount Dora Christian Academy's *Imagine* magazine (thank you Tim Deem). Also, the running text of the book contains a number of illustrative stories of good deeds from the Bible as well as more personal stories. And this retired rocket scientist also had to share a few illustrative stories from his career at NASA where appropriate.

One cannot write such a book and not also be impacted by it. I not only thank God for the opportunity and privilege to write it, but I am so appreciative of the shaping influence it has had on my life. To all my old and new friends who volunteered to let me interview you for the good deed stories—Thank You! The tears that some of you shed during the interviews continued as I put them together in story form. I pray your stories will impact the lives of the many people who will read them.

To Gayle Griffin and Steve Livermore, thank you for editing each chapter as I wrote them. Your thoughtful comments and corrections have made for a more readable book. I know the time and energy you expended took you away from your loved ones and personal interests, and I am forever grateful for your sacrifices in this regard.

I also want to thank Professor Allen Black, Dean at the Harding School of Theology, for clarifying a term in the Greek for me. I also want to continue to thank my many professors at this august graduate school, as you have contributed in so many ways to the person I am today.

Most of all, I thank my wife for tolerating my time away from her as I diligently wrote. Thank you for letting me read sections of the manuscript aloud to you throughout this long journey, especially at those times when you were worn out from a hard day at work. Also, I am most appreciative of the concepts we discussed and possible stories to include in the book.

Lastly, to the readers, I am thankful for the confidence you placed in me for purchasing and reading the book. I hope you will find that it was a confidence well placed. I can guarantee you that this book was a work of passion, prayed over, and well researched. I truly hope you enjoy it and find it spiritually enriching. I have already been praying for you that God will use this book to create in you a zeal for engaging in good deeds to address the pressing needs of others.

To my loving God, I praise Your holy name and offer thanksgiving and all the glory to You

CHAPTER 1

Divine Purpose

**The purpose in a man's heart is like deep water,
but a man of understanding will draw it out.**

(Prov. 20:5)[1]

Robert Mulholland tells an insightful story in his book, *Invitation to a Journey*, about a group of heroic individuals called the Rescue Society. Home to a reef-laden and rocky coast, the Rescue Society's purpose was to save the lives of the unfortunate seafarers whose ships struck a reef or rock off their treacherous shore. Through the years they saved hundreds of lives; nevertheless, this risky occupation occasionally took the life of one of the Society's own courageous rescuers.

As a new generation took over the reins, a fresh focus emerged. New technology and techniques seemed to offer the Society better approaches to their rescue efforts. They started to bring in consultants, attend workshops, and enjoy the visits of salespeople who touted their state-of-the-art equipment. Though saving lives remained their stated goal, another love stole their hearts and became their priority. Their techniques, preparation, and equipment developed into the primary focus of their efforts.

Then one night the unthinkable happened:

> ...while the entire Rescue Society was attending yet another meeting to perfect their rescue skills, a great passenger liner struck upon the reef and sank. Hundreds of people were lost because there was no one left to go to their rescue. The Rescue Society had come to exist for its own perfection and not for the sake of others.[2]

Purpose is crucial in our personal lives and in the lives of our churches. Purpose underpins our guiding visions. It helps us see future possibilities and desired outcomes. Its directional influence gives our activities a rudder to stay the course and navigate tricky waters. Purpose gives us the reason for our existence.

My experience with different churches has taught me that they can easily lose their God-given purposes for existence. As with the Rescue Society, they turn inward and become focused on the wrong priorities. Self-oriented desires take hold in various forms. You can hear the voices—"I want these types of songs in our worship service." "I want the Lord's Supper to be conducted in this particular way." "I want this program offered." "I want this taught or preached." I want, I want, I want. Nothing is wrong with expressing our desires, but self has a tendency of taking center stage. When this happens, we want "our" church, "our" way, not the Lord's church, His way.

Of course, the proper development of our inner-self is important but never at the expense or exclusion of the vertical and horizontal dimensions of our spirituality. If the development of self becomes our primary purpose, we may corrupt the image of Christ we desire to develop. Rather than "church" providing us an opportunity to grow our relationship with God (vertical) and become others-serving (horizontal), it is viewed as offering us knowledge for *self*-edification, techniques for *self*-improvement, *self*-gratifying worship experiences, and opportunities for *self*-promotion.

Like the Rescue Society, we can lose sight of the church's intended purpose. Our coming together week after week can begin to point inward, even though there are drowning souls all around us, surfacing for one last breath. One thing of which I am convicted is that our spiritual maturing and equipping is for the purpose of addressing the pressing needs of others. God's Word beckons us in this regard with purposeful language time and time again.

A Good Purpose

Paul desired to ground the fledgling church in Ephesus with the understanding that their salvation was a result of God's grace through His work in Christ Jesus. Their corresponding faith in this was paramount to their salvation, but their works did not contribute to it. What Christ did for us on the Cross can never be earned, only accepted as a gracious gift. Nevertheless, works become a core characteristic of those who walk in that grace.

> For by grace you have been saved through faith; and that not of yourselves, *it is* the gift of God; not as a result of works, so that no one may boast. For we are His workmanship, created in Christ Jesus for good works, which God prepared beforehand so that we would walk in them (Eph. 2:8-10).

Note how Paul wrote verse ten as a purpose statement. He succinctly stated that the workmanship God performed on His followers was for the intent of creating a people for the purpose of carrying out "good works." Good works define the life of the Christian. Conversely, a life devoid of good deeds stands in opposition to God's will for His people.

NASA created the Space Shuttle for the purpose of sending humans into space to facilitate its exploration. The appliance industry developed affordable microwave ovens for the purpose of heating foods quickly to revolutionize food preparation (one of my favorite inventions). Medical researchers created scopes to enter the human body for the purpose of decreasing the invasiveness of many medical procedures. God created us in Christ Jesus for the specific purpose of performing good deeds.

We can find a couple of other core purposes for God's people in Scripture, but it is to this divinely given purpose that this book devotes its pages.

God's Goodness

One beautiful Sunday in 2014, after morning worship services, I found myself in an emotional conversation with a dear friend and long-standing elder of our church. Many of my fellow brothers and sisters were busily heading to their cars but on this day I was oblivious to their presence. Even the joyful sound of the children playing could not penetrate the melancholy nature of our conversation.

He had recently received an upsetting diagnosis that a malignant cancerous growth had invaded his left maxillary sinus and had affected his left eye. Sadly, surgery was not an option, so to address the issue he would undergo radiation and chemotherapy. This fine man shared with me how a mask was created to fit and protect his face with an opening to allow the harmful rays of the radiation to pass through to the targeted area. While enduring the radiation treatment, it had taken a toll on him, as his mouth had erupted into painful sores. Tears then started to flow down his face as he asked me to pray for him, because he feared he may lose his left eye. Yet even while facing this fretful possibility, what this devoted elder emotionally expressed next caught me totally off guard. He three times fervently repeated, "Mike, God is good; God is good; God is so good!"

Many of us often use the expression, "God is good." Based on the context, this saying may take on various meanings. Obviously, it may simply be a declaration of God's goodness, but it often reflects something much deeper. For some, it is an expression of faith to carry on through troubled times because they trust in God's goodness. For others, this saying expresses gratitude for life's blessings. One friend aptly articulated use of this phrase from this perspective—this is "my heart's expression to verbally affirm that God's goodness transcends circumstances...it turns my focus to the eternal and away from the temporal." Our God is good, and believing and trusting that is important to our faith.

God's goodness comes in many different forms. Since God is holy, He is morally and ethically perfect and pure. God's integrity is incontestable. He is truthful and faithful and can be counted on to follow through on His promises. Fairness and justice are foundational to His approach to governing His creation.

God expresses His love toward us in many different ways. His benevolence seeks our ultimate welfare. His grace sees to our true needs and is based on His goodness not ours. His mercy sees us in a broken and pitiful condition and drives Him to action. And God's longsuffering nature puts up with a lot of our foolishness and brokenness, exhibiting undeserved patience with us. Yes, God is good.

Jesus demonstrated God's goodness in numerous ways. For example, we see Him reaching out to others in kindness in various capacities, such as healing the sick and casting demons out of the oppressed. He cared for the circumstances of the poor and society's downcasts. Jesus exhibited how living righteously was a matter of the heart, which produces godly behaviors. Ultimately, His unselfish act of love led Him to the cross to allow for the forgiveness of our sins, enabling us to have a new relationship with His Father.

Today, the gospel illuminates for us who God is in the life of Christ (2 Cor. 4:4). And through the Holy Spirit, God is at work in His people—transforming us into the likeness of His Son "from glory to glory" (2 Cor. 3:18). In other words, we are a work-in-progress. Our hearts are a divine construction zone, where our old selfish and worldly natures are being torn down, and upon the foundation of Christ Jesus, a heart based on the qualities of God's goodness is being rebuilt for His purposes. These hearts of goodness are not to be hoarded for our own selfish pursuits but for the sake of others. The fruit of these Spirit-formed hearts should be exhibited in our works for others.

Good Works

Work in the Greek carries with it a number of connotations. Work is purposeful, not aimless. It may consist of a simple act, a series of deeds, or be the actual product resulting from the work. Paul referred to a lengthy on-going work of God within the Christians at Philippi; "For I am confident of this very thing, that He who began a good work in you will perfect it until the day of Christ Jesus" (Phil. 1:6). Or in other words, our journey to become like Christ will be a progressive work of God until Jesus returns, and then He will complete it.[3]

I mention this because all good works are not created equal. Some may be simple one-time tasks, such as opening the door for someone who has her arms full. Some good deeds may require more time and effort, for example, building a playground for the children at your church. Other good deeds may be quite complex, requiring special skills, and perhaps long periods of time for the work to come to fruition. This might be the case with trying to help someone emotionally recover from the loss of a loved one.

The goal of good works is to bring the goodness of God into the lives of others. This should be a natural extension of who you are and never viewed as a behavioral requirement. Do not let any agendas be attached to your good works; the recipients of your actions should simply see that you care about them. Others will know we are of Christ by our expressions of love to them (Jn. 13:35). God will in turn open up the hearts of others to us through such genuinely caring behavior.

Good works will sometimes require sacrifice on our part; it is just the nature of the beast. Paul describes the attitude of those who are others-looking in Phil. 2:3-4:

> Do nothing from selfishness or empty conceit, but with humility of mind regard one another as more important than yourselves; do not *merely* look out for your own personal interests, but also for the interests of others.

A friend pointed out to me that "sacrifice is not always sacrificial." In other words, as our spirituality becomes fairly mature in certain facets of our Christian walk, what once was sacrificial now becomes second nature and no longer feels sacrificial. It is who we have become. And when a pressing need in the life of another crops up under particular situations, we virtually cannot help ourselves; we become compelled to give of ourselves to help meet the need. This is often seen in a mother's unwavering love for her children. This love causes her to meet her children's needs without any regard for her own requirements. Some circumstances will always confront us with a required sacrifice. However, as we grow, sacrifice will hopefully become less of a concern. Our spiritual maturity has truly progressed when a sacrifice given in the accomplishment of a good work becomes non-sacrificial in our minds.

I cannot over emphasize how important the performance of good deeds is to our spiritual development. If we truly want to become Christlike, serving others is a must. Looking out for the interests of others and acting on their needs will typically reinforce and progress the movements of our hearts in a Christlike direction. Their gratitude, expressions of appreciation, and even tears of joy can have a lasting impact on us and reinforce the value of our actions. Of course, dealing with people can sometimes be difficult and unpredictable, and we'll take quick look in the next chapter at how to handle the negatives we encounter.

Prepared Beforehand and Gifted

In Eph. 2:10, Paul tells us that God not only fashioned us after His Son to accomplish good works, He also has prepared in advance the works He desires of us. He does not force us to carry them out; we must "walk in them." Spirit-empowered, we are readied, the works are readied, and God relies on us to bring them to fruition. Andrew T. Lincoln explains, "It is grace all the way."

> To say that God has prepared the good works in advance in his sovereign purpose is also to stress in the strongest possible way that believers' good deeds cannot be chalked up to their own resolve, but are due solely to divine grace.[4]

Saved by grace; now let's walk by grace and carry out the divine purpose set before us by our loving God. Perhaps like me, you have felt a burning desire to carry out a particular good work in the life of another, and nothing seems to quench it. What else should we expect when such a work was created for "yours truly."

And if that's not enough, our loving God wants to make sure that He specifically equips you for works of service.

> As each one has received a special gift, employ it in serving one another, as good stewards of the manifold grace of God (1 Pet. 4:10).

You cannot choose your gift; it was given especially to you by the grace of God. Nevertheless, God has given you control as when to use it. You are its steward and a "good" one if you utilize it for the purpose of serving others. It appears logical to me that part of God's workmanship in creating you anew includes imparting you this grace gift. And it follows that He expects you to use it for those good works He has prepared just for you.

For the gifted encourager, whether you find out someone is down-and-out, has overcome a past life issue, or has accomplished something meaningful, you will likely be confronted with a circumstance, where a deep-seated passion will overtake you to put your gift into action. After administering a good dose of care and support, you will hopefully walk away uplifted. In God's grace, you were prepared, you were gifted, and the work was prepared for you. Now our gracious God can go to work on a heart He has impacted through your service. Absolutely, "Grace all the way!" Now let's go be gracious.

A Beautiful Thing

I believe William M. Golden's words in the old hymn "A Beautiful Life" truly express the Christian life in regard to our reaching out to others. The first and fourth verses get to the heart of the matter.

> Each day I'll do a golden deed,
> By helping those who are in need;
> My life on earth is but a span,

And so I'll do the best I can...

While going down life's weary road,
I'll try to lift some trav'ler's load;
I'll try to turn the night to day,
Make flowers bloom along the way...[5]

Golden does not include the phrase "a beautiful life" in the actual song, but did he ever nail it with the title. Replacing others' darkness with light, turning life's weariness into flowering goodness, and seeking to help the needy—those are golden deeds. That's our lot in life! Yes, that's a beautiful life!

▪ GOOD DEEDS TO PONDER

At the end of each chapter, I will provide you with a good work or two to think over and perhaps spur you to ask yourself a few questions. Can you picture yourself doing such a good work? Did this good work spark a passion within you? If you changed the circumstances could this be an area in which you could serve? What gift(s) do you see at work? Do you see yourself gifted in this area or a similar one? What would it take for you to start performing such good deeds and under what circumstances?

A Touch of Compassion

Years ago, an operating room nurse decided she was going to do her job a little differently. Her role as circulating nurse required her to be with the patient facing surgery throughout the process; before the operation, during the operation, and after the operation. While other nurses might have been a little more matter-of-fact in their approach as they discussed the upcoming surgery with their patient, she talked with the patient differently. She viewed the patient, not as a surgical object, but a fretful human being with little control as to what lay ahead for them.

Her goal was to make her patients comfortable with their procedure and as free of fear as possible. So rather than standing over the patient and asking a series of questions and going through the usual procedural mumbo jumbo, she pulled up a chair alongside the patient's bed to help put him at ease and actually talked him through his concerns. She went through the information that was required, but she also extended her hand alongside his and asked about his fears and worries.

Often, patients took hold of her hand and poured out their anxieties and fears. Her goal was to do something "for" them, not "to" them, so in her tenderhearted way she gave reassurance and brought understanding and support to them.

Because of her compassionate touch, many asked, "Are you a Christian?" And she humbly responded that she was. For some of these patients, knowing that one of God's own looked over them was a source of encouragement. Even in those few hours that she touched the lives of her patients, she came close to them. By empathizing and walking alongside them, she created a bond of care for those under her charge. She was using her God-given gifts to serve and be a positive influence for the Lord.

Impeccable Timing

One Sunday morning, I remember feeling a little down because I had been questioning some of my life decisions. Worship services had just concluded, and I had weaved my way through my fellow brothers and sisters back to the foyer. While still among a throng of people, a kind longtime friend took hold of my arm from behind and drew close to me. She then leaned forward and said in an enthusiastic tone,

"I just finished reading your book [*An Angel's View*] for the third time." I thanked her for sharing that with me, hugged her, and off she went smiling.

On the surface, one might think, *Well that was a kind thing to say,* but it was really so much more. I can testify unequivocally that those words brought reassurance to the core of my being. As an author, for someone to tell you she spent her precious time reading your book three times communicates volumes. For her, something of value entered her life that was worthy of mining for its spiritual gems and nuggets. Tearfully, later that day, I remember feeling a sense of validation that all the research, writing, rewriting, and prayers for guidance were truly worth it. God was using my book to draw others to Him and help them in their spiritual walk. My godly purpose was confirmed and strengthened.

This God-sent, Spirit-driven woman probably did not really know how her encouraging words would impact me, but she did realize that such a comment needed to be shared. Targeted by a gifted encourager, those words penetrated deep and were filled with uplifting power. Sometimes just saying the simplest positive thing may hold the deepest of meaning for another person. To me, such actions are at the heart of being Christian. Now let's encourage and uplift one another.

Questions

1. What core purposes deeply guide your daily walk?

2. How might our church's God-given purposes become skewed because of "self"? How might our spirituality be impacted?

3. Have you ever considered that one of God's core purposes for you is to perform good works? What will you need to change in your life to incorporate this purpose anew or at a deeper level?

4. Survey your recent past and determine what good deeds have been done for you? What type of impact did they have on you personally?

5. Why do you think God desires you to perform good works for others?

6. If God has "prepared beforehand" good works for you to be involved in and a gift(s) to serve others in that regard, are you following through on what God has provided you? Are there good deeds probing at your heart that you are attracted to performing? What does that suggest?

CHAPTER 2

Keeping the Light On

**But the path of the righteous is like the light of dawn,
That shines brighter and brighter until the full day.**

(Prov. 4:18)

One of the great perks of working on the Space Shuttle Program included watching an occasional launch from just three-and-a-half miles away. When my role for the launch countdown consisted of supporting the loading of propellants into the External Tank, I was released around three hours before liftoff once the launch team reported for duty. Typically on those occasions, I hung around and kept up with the countdown from my office.

At T-minus twenty (T-20) minutes and counting, I bolted from my office and went directly to the vicinity of the Launch Control Center to watch the launch. Precisely at 6.6 seconds before liftoff, the Shuttle's flight computers would start the first main engine, then 120 milliseconds apart the next two were started. With three good engines up and running, the Solid Rocket Boosters were ignited at T-0. "Spectacular" only begins to describe what I then witnessed, Wow! Jumping off the launch pad, the Shuttle's propulsions systems produced a radiant and stunning plume leaving a stream of exhaust gases behind that extended to its previously serene resting place.

Experiencing the acoustic shock wave in such close proximity to the launch pad may have been the high point, but as this space-bound behemoth ascended through the atmosphere, one quickly became mesmerized by the light of the plume. And at night, the dark starry sky became brilliantly illuminated. On one occasion during a night launch, a haze hung over the Space Coast. When the Shuttle streamed upward, its plume literally set the haze around us aglow as the light eerily refracted through it. It was absolutely stunning!

My friends from the other side of Florida have shared with me that on clear days they could see Shuttle launches from their distant area. Even if we wanted to hide what we were up to at the Kennedy Space Center (KSC), the light of the Shuttle's plume would have quickly revealed our endeavors.

Let it Shine

Jesus knew darkness can easily engulf our world and during the Sermon on the Mount, He encouraged His disciples to shine brightly by bringing goodness into the lives of others.

> You are the light of the world. A city set on a hill cannot be hidden. Nor do men light a lamp, and put it under the peck-measure, but on the lampstand; and it gives light to all who are in the house. Let your light shine before men in such a way that they may see your good works, and glorify your Father who is in heaven (Matt. 5:14-16).

Jesus emphatically told His disciples that "you are the light of the world." Not the rulers, Jews, or great philosophers of the day—His disciples. In our contemporary times, the spotlight might temporarily shine on certain individuals, but our politicians, news reporters, Hollywood stars, or sports heroes are still not "the light"—God's people are.

Several years back, a minister friend of mine in Three Forks, Montana took Carol and me to the Lewis and Clark Caverns. After the guide took us into the depths of the cavern system, he stopped our group and prepared us for an unexpected feature of the tour. He then turned out the lights. An eerie and uneasy feeling quickly overwhelmed us, as it was pitch black. No light seeped in from anywhere. Our eyes vainly tried to adjust to the darkness but fully dilated pupils are useless in absolute darkness. However, my sense of hearing was working quite well, as the click of the switch sounded like a clap of thunder, when the guide turned the lights back on. Reflecting on this experience, it truly helps me to appreciate Jesus' power to penetrate spiritual darkness and the relief His glorious light brings to a darkened soul. Please let that light shine!

Since Jesus was "the light of the world" (Jn. 8:12), when we follow Him we "become sons of light" (Jn. 12:36). And in Matthew 5, Jesus basically concludes the obvious: Since we are light, it is our gracious duty to shine; light's very nature is to be seen. Paul stated it this way to the Ephesian Christians:

> ...you were formerly darkness, but now you are light in the Lord; walk as children of light (for the fruit of the light consists in all goodness and righteousness and truth)" (Eph. 5:8-9).

Or more directly and in my words, "People of light produce works of light."

An Uneasy Tension

Ancient towns were often built on hills of white limestone, and like the radiant plume of a Shuttle after liftoff, the city conspicuously stood out as it gleamed in the pure light of the sun. With lamps and torches burning at night, the city on a hill was evident from a distance.[6] Jesus' example would have thoroughly resonated with His disciples. As "lights," they must shine brightly for others to see and not remain hidden.

Jesus drives His point home with another well-understood example. The old VBS song fully grasps what to do and not do with a lit lamp; "Hide it under a bushel—NO! I'm gonna' let it shine." Essentially Jesus was saying, "Now would it not be absurd to light a lamp only to cover it up so no light comes from it? No, you place the lamp on a high stand to obtain the utmost benefit from its illuminating quality."

Do you think we should ever choose to quench our God-given lights? You might ask, "But what about humility, are not Christians supposed to develop humble hearts? Does not shining brightly potentially place us in the grips of temptation?" In fact,

Jesus warns His listeners just a short time later in the Sermon on the Mount that they must avoid the desire to be noticed and honored by others when performing acts of righteousness (Matt. 6:1-6).

While at NASA, I knew a number of individuals who constantly wanted to "toot their own horns" and show how great they were in front of management and their colleagues. Their true nature was evident, and they often manipulated situations and others to receive their perceived accolades. Nevertheless, Jesus wants our lights to be shining so others will take notice of our good works (Matt. 5:16). Yet He revealed in the second half of the verse the purpose of this shining behavior; it is to "glorify your Father who is in heaven." Our works are about God, not us. When they become about us, then we need to turn our light off and perform our good works in private. A preacher once told me that "you know you have a problem when you pat yourself on the back so hard that you almost break your arm." He then wistfully added, "Oh by the way, you just received your only reward in doing so." Kidding aside, if you struggle with humility, please begin praying for this vital trait and start putting others first. We need more individuals shining brightly in this gloomy world. So yes, Jesus wants your good works done out in the open, but only while maintaining a humble attitude internally.

I have known a number of individuals who want to do their good deeds behind the scenes or remain anonymous. There may be times when such a course of action is prudent. For example, when helping someone work through certain spiritual issues, especially when it involves others, discretion may be necessary to avoid revealing hurtful facts about all concerned. Always remember, some brothers and sisters are tempted to gossip when presented with certain information. Also, giving money to others in need may also require a private approach for a couple of different reasons. Jesus actually mentioned this particular good work as one that would best be conducted in private (Matt. 6:2-4).

But in general, Jesus wants us to bring our good deeds into the light. God formed you in the image of His Son for the purpose of carrying out good works—works He prepared for you; works He gifted you to perform. Be true to your nature, turn your "light" on and honor God by humbly fulfilling your purpose.

Glorious Results

Many wonderful results can occur when you perform good works to honor God. For one, Jesus wants the world to know that we are His disciples.

> A new commandment I give to you, that you love one another, even as I have loved you, that you also love one another. By this all men will know that you are My disciples, if you have love for one another (Jn. 13:34-35).

Note that this loving is observed by "all men," occurring out in the open for all to see. Such love goes far beyond just a feeling. Others see the loving ways Christ's disciples treat and care for one another, and by this, others can deduce that you are Jesus' disciples. Perhaps they might even like to become one as well.

Secondly, before you came to Christ, those close to you knew what you valued and how you led your life. With Christ as your Savior and a new light shining from a heart undergoing transformation, they hopefully will notice a change. Just like the Shuttle's plume in the sky unmistakably reveals what NASA's is up to, your good works will shine a light on your newly acquired values and character traits: values that hold God in a loving embrace and esteem the needs of others even over your own. Perhaps the captivated onlookers might like to know more about your change.

Moreover, God is working *in* you and *through* you in your good works. Like the Apostle Paul, you may have weaknesses in your life that might normally stand in the way of accomplishing certain things. But Paul found strength in those weaknesses. The power of Christ was richly alive in him and helped him to accomplish what he did in Corinth. By seeing Paul's "weaknesses," the Corinthians

25

knew that God must have been at work in Paul's ministry to give the results that they had personally witnessed. Today, others may also see God working through your weaknesses to accomplish what might have once been thought of as unimaginable. Perhaps they might like to know more about this God who is working through you.

Additionally, many people are far too acquainted with the horrible results that stem from a society held in the grips of selfishness, violence, indifference, and dishonesty. Observing your good deeds may provide hope. Some may see a better way to live with one another. A way where love reigns in the hearts of God's people, producing acts of kindness, gentleness, and mercy. They see you loving your neighbor as yourself, when you come to the aid of those with pressing needs. A vision of life comes into view for them where trust and goodness dictate behavior. Perhaps these enlightened observers will want to know what motivates you to live life in such a gracious fashion.

Lastly, others may see your unselfish works and develop a desire to carry out such good deeds themselves. Members of a central Florida church recently painted nine houses in their community for families that could not afford to do so themselves. During preparation, painting, and clean-up, a few of the family members of these homes became acquainted with some of these service-minded workers. They soon recognized that they were the beneficiaries of a selfless act of love, so three of the nine families decided to start attending this church. The preacher told me, "Their attendance was not some passing form of appreciation. They genuinely wanted to be a part of this good work and paint the homes of other needy families in the future." The light at-tracted them, may "The Light" come to dwell in them.

Even a prophet of old was personally impacted and grateful for the good deeds of a caring individual. Elisha frequently passed by the house of a prominent woman in Shunem who was able to offer him hospitality, so when he traveled close to her home "he turned in there to eat" (2 Kings 4:8). She perceived something was different about Elisha, she stated "this is a holy man of God" (v.9). Richard Nelson notes that "she is not recognizing any moral virtue but the aura of power...of one who is in close contact with God."[7]

The Shunamite woman persuaded her husband to build a room for this godly passer-by. The text suggests that this was not a temporary structure, but a fully furnished, permanent dwelling probably built on their roof.[8] Elisha was so appreciative of the care she extended to him and his servant that he offered to do something for her. However, her good deed came from a caring heart not one looking for something in return, so she was not interested in his offer. Nonetheless, Elisha appeared determined to show his gratitude, and his servant astutely noted that "she has no son and her husband is old" (v. 14). Now the power of God residing in this holy man became truly evident to the woman when he promised her a baby boy. In this ancient setting, this was a joyous gift to a woman, as she could fulfill her primary role of providing an heir for her husband. Now that's an amazing good deed in response to her initial gracious acts. Good deeds tend to promote more good deeds.

Some additional reasons may come to mind as to why we should perform our good works publicly; but I think from the story above you can understand the value of doing so. Some of the above may sound somewhat idealistic, but we must recognize that we are a work in progress. A little bungling and miscalculating by us as humans may occur, but we need to keep pressing on to that ideal. Our lights will become brighter, and others will appreciate basking in the warmth of the glow.

Keep the Light Burning
Keeping the light on is often easier said than done. Age, criticism, illness, and the like tend to easily douse our flames. Resurrecting that old VBS song again, we should be ever vigilant when it comes

to our flames—"Don't let Satan blow it out! I'm gonna' let it shine." If that song is echoing away in your head by now, maybe that's a good thing.

When she was about 80, my mother went into a nursing home with a severely debilitating case of rheumatoid arthritis. Her rheumatologist once noted that she and another man had the two worst cases he had ever encountered. My dear mother's life was one of pain management at that point, and she needed twenty-four hour nursing care available. One godly man from my church took the time to visit her occasionally and read her the Bible. After church one night, he came to me humbly and said, "I visit your mom to encourage her, but the truth of the matter is that I am the one being encouraged." My mom was a fighter and full of faith; her light would not be extinguished. She encouraged others until the day she passed.

Criticism, either verbally or by action, is hurtful when it concerns our good deeds. For many of us, we choose to let others extinguish our light rather than to experience the hurt again. Through the years, I have seen criticism and hurtful acts take their toll on good deed doers again and again. They often in disgust declare, "Well, I am never going to help with this again." Can you imagine having a conversation with God over this? "God, brother Yappy made this horrible comment about my labor of love so I am never going to serve You again in this capacity." I'm not sure such a response would please our heavenly Father. Serving Him is not about pleasing everyone else. Just prior to Jesus' declaration that His disciples were "the light of the world," He warned them that persecution and insults would come. Dealing with hurt is never easy, but Jesus actually bids us to rejoice because "your reward in heaven is great" (Matt. 5:12).

Remember, our good works are about our service to God. Others may not appreciate or be mindful of our works, but the author of Hebrews reminds us that our God powerfully remembers the quality and intent of our service.

For God is not unjust so as to forget your work and the love which you have shown toward His name, in having ministered and in still ministering to the saints. And we desire that each show the same diligence so as to realize the full assurance of hope until the end, that you may not be sluggish, but imitators of those who through faith and patience inherit the promises (Heb. 6:10-12).

God is just and will remember our works, but He wants us to remain diligent and not slow down in carrying out the good works He has prepared for us. When we "keep on keeping on" no matter who criticizes us or whatever occurs, we can grasp the full assurance of the hope of our inheritance. Let's keep those lights burning for all to see, and as that old VBS song aptly reminds us: "Let it shine, all the time, let it shine!"

■ GOOD DEEDS TO PONDER

The first good deed story for your reflection involves a lovely woman who refused to let age and health be an impediment to blessing others. The next is the first of a few corporate-level good works stories I will include. Good works involving a large portion of a congregation provide a nice training ground to develop passion to serve others. May your lights be lit!

Keep on Blessing

With her eyesight degrading, a sad day came when an outgoing and caring woman could no longer drive. Sad, not because she lost the privilege to drive, but it was her means for blessing others. After her husband suffered a stroke in 1992, this veteran of forty years in the mission field retired from this gracious work and earnestly sought a new avenue to bless others. Knowing how richly blessed she was by the Lord, blessing others became paramount in her life. Her car turned into her life-blood to visit shut-ins, the sick and those in nursing homes, as well as taking elderly friends to the grocery store and the doctor. Blessing others was imprinted on her DNA and losing the ability to drive was a devastating blow.

She yearned for a new avenue to bring goodness into the lives of others. Recalling how a man's ministry blessed her and her husband many years prior, she had a wonderful idea. She would become "Birthday Betty." With a list of birthdays from her Equipping Minister and a church directory, this 85 year old harbinger of birthday greetings now brings love and well wishes to each of her congregation's members on their special day. With her gifts of communicating and connecting with others, the telephone now serves as her new means of blessing the members of her congregation. Many truly appreciate her calls and seek her out at church to express their gratitude in person. But perhaps most of all, she really enjoys listening to the excited voices of the children talk about their birthday parties. For her, blessing is a blessing. I think every church needs a "Birthday Betty."

She also has shared her experiences in the mission field with many of the children's classes at her congregation, hoping to produce a love for bringing the Gospel to others in these young hearts. The fifth graders showed such an interest with her proficiency in working with the Japanese that she has continued to share with them for a few minutes each class some nuances of the Japanese language. What a wonderful way to help develop young hearts to care for people in other cultures and produce a future generation who desires to bless others. Never stop being a blessing!

Community Counts

If you were out for a drive around Ocala, Florida on two particular Saturdays of 2015, you might have come across a beehive of activity around two homes and two local help agencies. Planted proudly at each site for all eyes to see were signs that read, "Community Counts—Out of the Pews and Into the Community." Now that's not something you see every day. A local area church mobilized 140 of its 180 members to tackle four projects in its city. Painters, preparers, food servers, runners, photographers, house cleaners, lawn beautifiers, and toy repairers were rallied to take on these two day works of goodness. To fund this good work, the church took up a special contribution on each first Sunday of the month for "God and my neighbor." Nine sponsors also chipped in as well, with money and resources.

At the Women's Pregnancy Center, volunteers pressure washed the fascia and walkway, along with cleaning the windows and several rooms inside the facility. By serving this center, the church wanted to show its support for their mission and walk alongside them in valuing the sanctity of life. The faith-filled workers desired to free-up the center's staff and allowed it to use its limited resources to work directly with their clients in need.

The work accomplished at the Domestic Violence Center's (DVC) live-in shelter involved painting two of the many bedrooms that house up to four dozen guests and a 120 foot hallway. Volunteers organized and cleaned the center's pantry and playroom, and they repaired several broken toys. And perhaps the most fun, a few of the teens played with some of the center's children during all the commotion.

With lights shining brightly, these benevolent workers came to understand the meaningful roles of these Centers and how lives are impacted by their work. They came face-to-face with the hard lives some people endure, and such awareness has a way of reshaping hearts. Perhaps the greatest reward came at the banquet for the workers, sponsors, and Centers' staff, when a woman from the DVC sincerely stated, "This has restored my faith in God." She surely witnessed some dazzling "lights."

At the two private residences, the activities became a little more personal with the families as workers prepped and painted the houses, along with performing some lawn maintenance. Conversations started as a couple of residents gratefully joined in the tasks at hand. Poverty had not taken away their will to work. The church's youth minister started chatting with the grandson at one of the homes and before long the young man asked the minister if he would perform his wedding ceremony. He graciously accepted as long as they allowed him to counsel them prior to their exchanging vows. When the banquet was held, members from both families attended and expressed deep gratitude for the loving gifts they received. One 83 year-old lady said, "I am so happy I could dance." And so she did!

Out from the comfort of the pews, many hearts grew in wonderful ways through this endeavor. Fueled by personal sacrifice, new relationships, intergenerational service, and witnessing heartfelt gratitude, the organizer accomplished his goal of helping some of his good deed doers become more like Jesus.

Questions

1. Jesus wants His disciples to shine brightly before the world with their good works. Is that a problem for you? If so, why and how might you change?

2. When might performing a good deed in the light become a problem? What course of action should you take?

3. Along with glorifying God, how might your good works be beneficial to a dark world?

4. What good works do you think should be accomplished discreetly? And why is that the case? List several good works that typically can be done in public.

5. What impediments exist that might extinguish your light? Have any of these caused you to ever stop serving God in the past? How might you handle those impediments differently today?

6. Explain the role of humility in performing your good works.

CHAPTER 3

Called as Zealots

**Likewise also, deeds that are good are quite evident,
and those which are otherwise cannot be concealed.**

(1 Tim. 5:25)

Convicted that his past teaching on a particular qualification for elders and deacons contained an incorrect conclusion, a preacher knew the time had come to set things straight. Names of potential new elders and deacons were going before the congregation for their approval, and he recognized his changed view might create some anxiety. So the preacher and the existing elders prayerfully studied the passages of concern together and came to total agreement on the subject. He was given leadership's blessing to explain this corrected position on the qualification to the congregation. After the presentation, rumblings of discord immediately started, but when the specific names for the new leaders went forward, the reality of the new teaching caused a small group of individuals to factiously react. They called others and stirred them up to withdraw their support from the church's existing leadership and to derail the placement of some of the candidates for elders and deacons. As a result, an ugly furor erupted, and about fifty people left the church that year. Backbiting, name calling, criticizing and hurt feelings became the norm.

About a year later, multiple Christian universities were consulted on the toxic subject. The preacher and leadership's interpretation was validated, so they revisited the passages with their membership. Another list of willing servants was brought before the congregation for consideration as elders and deacons. Not surprisingly turmoil broke out again. This sadly resulted in fifty more people leaving the church that year. One man who was ready to serve the church in a new leadership capacity was personally devastated. Even visitors were not immune to the contentious conduct, as one instigator discouraged their return by saying, "We have problems at this church." Drugged with self-righteous indignation, the agitators demanded the resignation of the preacher and wanted to seize control from the elders. After a short time, it was evident they would not succeed, so the divisive members finally left.

For a two- to three-year period, this church utterly stalled. It was virtually paralyzed by the caustic tenor of those days, and per the preacher, "Nothing good happened." Have you ever been to that church?

Why begin a chapter titled "Called as Zealots" with such a negative story? Because for good works to thrive in a church; the factious, rebellious, and quarrelsome behavior of some brothers and sisters *must* be stopped to accomplish our core purpose of performing good deeds.

Trouble in Crete

After initially establishing a number of churches in Crete, Paul's mission work called him elsewhere, so he left Titus to "set in order what remains" and "appoint elders in every city" (Titus 1:5). Paul became aware that these start-up congregations were experiencing trouble, so he wrote a letter to Titus to address their precarious circumstances. Subsequent to outlining the qualifications for elders in his letter (vv. 1:6-9), Paul immediately revealed his concerns for the Cretan churches and the pressing need for choosing leaders.

> For there are many rebellious men, empty talkers and deceivers, especially those of the circumcision, who must be silenced because they are upsetting whole families, teaching things they should not teach for the sake of sordid gain (Titus 1:10-11).

Chaos held these churches in its dark clutches. Apparently, some of the Jewish converts had displaced the truths of the Gospel with ritualistic matters from the old Law and imposed their traditions as commandments on these fledgling congregations (see 1:14-15 and 3:9). Paul described these legalistic perpetrators as those "who turn away from the truth" (v. 1:14). Gordon D. Fee aptly summarizes the idea behind Paul's statement as "...meaning the rejection of the Gospel [sic], whose 'good news' of salvation by grace stands in sharp contrast to all forms of religious rules and regulations."[9]

The end result was that these greed-driven, false teachers were misleading the Cretan Christians by their fallacious teachings and "upsetting whole families" along with creating disharmony and factions (vv. 3:9-10). The Greek term for "families" could be translated as "households," and since these were house churches, Paul may be concerned that these errant teachings were negatively impacting whole house churches.[10]

Whatever the case, Paul wanted Titus and the new leadership to "silence" (v. 1:11) these false teachers and to "reprove them severely" (v. 13). It's worthy of noting that Paul's motivation was not one of punishing these agitators, but "that they may be sound in the faith" (v. 13). Nevertheless, if individuals chose to continue to cause divisions after two warnings, Paul instructed Titus to reject them and have nothing to do with their antics. Basically, such behavior was sinful, and the ones who chose to go down that path had turned aside from the faith (vv. 3:10-11).

Starting in 1:16, Paul's letter to Titus started to turn into an exposition on good deeds and Christian conduct. Paul knew the factious behavior of the false teachers prevented the Christians in the Cretan churches from accomplishing their core purpose of performing good deeds. Unfortunately, I have experienced the harmful atmosphere of a church caught up in divisive behavior. When you are personally belittled and misrepresented, your mind sadly does not tend to focus on the needs of others. Perhaps only the purest of good deed doers can push onward through such a cold-hearted landscape.

I recently was out for a run at a park in Florida and came across two medium-sized gators who were engaged in the midst of a tussle. One gator had the other one's tail in its mouth, and not liking being chomped on, the second gator had curled backward in an attempt to return the favor by biting its oppressor's tail. While running past this twisted mass of gator, I quickly realized nobody was winning and nobody was losing. It kind of reminded me of some factious situations I've experienced in churches through the years. Trading bite for bite, brothers and sisters staunchly took their side on some divisive issue. And of course, nobody was winning, but in this case, "everybody" was losing. Peacemaking and seeking unity was not on their radar screens. Paul warned the Galatians of the potentiality of such behavior; "But if you bite and devour one another, take care that you are not consumed by one another" (Gal. 5:15).

At this point, I would like to make an appeal to you who serve as leaders in your congregations. Apparent from a study of Titus, one of your God-given responsibilities is to assure that your members can live out their purpose of performing good works. Actions by your members that produce disputes and factions need to be quickly addressed and stopped. There are times when elders may decide to let certain caustic situations run their course to see if they would work themselves out. Unfortunately, such a tactic is typically unwise as most circumstances like these tend to continue to degrade. Creating and sustaining an environment where good works can flourish is a principal function of church leadership. Though unenviable, it's a noble task. Serve well and lead by also carrying out good deeds of your own. Others will notice and desire to follow.

You might be wondering why I included Titus 1:16 as part of Paul's exposition of good deeds because of its negative tenor. But that is exactly why it is important, as Paul vividly points out the result of misleading and divisive behavior.

> They profess to know God, but by their deeds they deny Him, being detestable and disobedient, and worthless for any good deed (Titus 1:16).

What a sad state of affairs! They claimed to "know God," but their deeds testified against them. They claimed purity but were detestable. They imposed obedience to man-made regulations but were actually disobedient to "the truth." Paul left no question as to their value for their created purpose of conducting good works—they were *worthless*. One of the major problems that plagues churches today is that so many individuals outwardly claim Christianity as their faith but live abhorrent lifestyles.

When I researched for NASA how the Agency might provide spiritual support for its astronauts, I gathered information on their spiritual needs in relation to their missions. My investigation was accomplished through various sources, including some interviews. I remember one astronaut who did not claim to be religious but seemed concerned as to whether some of his fellow space travelers presented themselves as Christians. To him, they might maintain they were Christians, but by living in such close quarters with some of them for an extended period of time, their conduct stated otherwise. I understood his point and have no reason to doubt his assessment. A considerable number of the men and women who have passed through the astronaut corps, however, were not only individuals of great courage and intellect, but many were of great faith as well. Nevertheless, this astronaut's appraisal should concern us all, because many individuals believe Christians lead hypocritical lives and want nothing to do with us or our churches.

Though people are at different stages in their spiritual maturity, all are fallible, and all continue to sin now and then. If we constantly behave like those in the world, why would others desire to join us? Hopefully the majority of our behaviors demonstrate that we are living transformed lives. By definition, Christians are "holy ones" (saints) and are to be holy like their God, and we must live out our holiness in the world. If we want people to join our ranks, then we must act like our gracious God who saved us by exhibiting lives of love, compassion, and integrity. What are you communicating by your actions?

Christ's Own Personal Zealots

Several reasons lay behind the writing of this book, but none greater than the profound impact the following verse had on my heart. Paul presented in the following passage the theological foundation for why good works should characterize the Christian. In referring to Christ, Paul said,

> ...who gave Himself for us, that He might redeem us from every lawless deed, and to purify for Himself a people for His own possession, zealous for good deeds (Titus 2:14).

I hope this verse speaks to your heart like it does mine. Jesus' love-driven sacrifice on the cross results in two life-giving outcomes when we turn to Him. First, because He paid the price for our transgressions with His life, He liberates us from the bondage of sin. Second, He purifies us (or makes us holy) by the blood He shed for us. Our newfound holiness allows us to enter into a new relationship with our Savior and God. And because He redeemed us, we are now Christ's own!

In MercyMe's contemporary Christian song, *Spoken For*, the songwriter imagined that he overheard Jesus pointing him out and stating, "This one's mine." Because of Christ's remarkable love for him, the captivated singer joyfully responded by proclaiming, "My heart is spoken for." We need to wrap our minds around this thought and let it ooze into the recesses of our hearts. We are Christ's own! We are spoken for! Our identity lies securely in His loving embrace, if we allow it.

How should we respond to Jesus' love for us? With thankfulness, thankfulness, thankfulness! Jesus paid a tremendous price for us, so in loving gratitude, our hearts should produce not only a passionate willingness to follow Him, but a zealous spirit to perform the good deeds His Father has prepared for us. If such passion and zeal have never truly formed in you, you might want to question whether you are truly thankful for what Christ accomplished for you on the cross. Has your Christian life been more about you or about what Christ has done for you? Perhaps your ultimate concern is in following rules rather than letting Christ form in you. Note how the origin of the deeds of the zealot's and Cretan agitators' stood in stark contrast in Titus. The zealot's good works came from a heart-changing understanding of the redemptive work of Christ, whereas the agitator's human-derived legalistic beliefs created hard hearts "worthless for any good deed."[11]

Zeal is not whimsical. It stems from an intense devotion to a cause or belief. Knowing our loving Savior desires for us to reach out to others by helping them meet the pressing needs in their lives should produce zeal within us. His aspirations for us ought to become our life's focus as we gratefully respond to His redemptive and sacrificial love. In no uncertain terms, Christians should be good deed *zealots*.

NASA is a unique government agency in its ability to attract a passionate workforce. From the early ages of childhood, many of my colleagues dreamed of someday working for the agency that explores the mysteries of space. And you must admit, not many children say, "Wow, I can't wait to go to work for the IRS!" or "Working for the Social Security Administration, now that's for me." NASA's allure of launching humans and robots into the unknown reaches of space is quite exciting, and I can personally attest that many of my co-workers were enthusiastic space zealots. In a similar manner, Jesus wants to launch His people on a trajectory to zealously help others.

One of my good friends is the most enthusiastic good deeds

zealot I have ever known. I have seen him help alcoholics, drug addicts, the unemployed, those just released from jail, and those incapacitated due to illness, just to name a few. He and his wife even welcomed into their home a man with a terminal illness to provide him a place to die in dignity. He loves people and deeply yearns to help them work through the problems they face. If we can find a sliver of this type of zeal, we can truly make a difference in this world for God.

Perhaps the biggest enemy to the development of a good deed zealot is indifference. "The indifferent" is virtually devoid of care. The needs of others produce no action only slight notice and may not be much more than an annoyance. The personal pursuits of "the indifferent" always win out over someone else's needs. Their business interests, recreation, entertainment, sports, and other activities are their priority, and others shouldn't dare to intrude on them. Sacrifice is not a concept they embrace. The spirituality of "the indifferent" is horribly corrupt. As Peter says, "Even so faith, if it has no works, is dead, being by itself" and "is useless" (James 2:17 and 20). True Christian faith must care about the misfortune of others and bring about action. Indifference is a scourge on the 21st-century church and must be recognized and dealt with for what it produces—dead Christians.

Indifference, though, does have a positive side. When one is indifferent to whom they reach out, strike one up for this ambiguous quality. There is a wonderful woman at my church who takes good advantage of this type of indifference. Whenever a family loses a loved one or is devastated by an illness, she responds to such news as a call-to-duty. She immediately organizes meals to be taken to their home and joins by lovingly preparing something sumptuous for them. She mentioned to me that when such grievous news occurs, a "burning passion to do something" rises up within her. She said that during stressful circumstances, "It means so much when people help." When it comes to understanding the positive impact of good deeds, life has been a tough training ground for her. She has experienced more than her share of difficulties. At 14, she lost her mother to a car accident involving a drunk driver. Through her married years, she fretfully helped her teenage daughter battle cancer, endured her son's six surgeries, lost their home to a devastating fire, and rallied round her husband when he lost a finger. Stress confronted her head-on on multiple occasions but because of the loving care of others, that stress became manageable. She now seeks ways to remove the stress from others by taking some of life's daily burdens off their shoulders. To her, such good deeds are a little thing, but to those impacted, it means a lot. And I can attest to her caring nature, since her grace and zeal have come my way on more than one occasion.

We should not put God's good deed zealots in a box that only serves humankind. All creation was impacted by the Fall. Paul stated that creation groans and suffers because of its subjection to futility and corruption (Rom. 8:18-22). When chiding Jonah, God in a question basically told His disgruntled prophet that His compassion was not only for the wayward Ninevites, but for their animals as well (Jon. 4:11). So we should not be surprised when we see a remarkable zeal in the hearts of some people for the plight of animals or the environment in this world. God surely has instilled a passion within them to care for His creation in a special way.

I know one young woman whose fondness for stray cats is a driving force in her life. She rescues these distressed felines from our roadways, storm drains, and vacant fields. Abandoned to die, sick, and infested with parasites, these cats would most likely die without her benevolence. This Good Samaritan of cats takes them to the vet, nurtures them back to health, and helps her furry friends find good homes. She also provides free marketing services to a cat rescue agency and fosters cats to prepare them for adoption, avoiding needless euthanization. Fostering cats may sound like fun but many are recovering from illnesses or surgeries and need a lot of care, as well as a little housebreaking. If cats could talk, some would tearfully share stories of compassion, and how this remarkable woman sacrificially loved on them and gave them a second chance at life.

Role Models

In Titus 2, Paul shifted his focus to a more positive nature and started sharing the attributes of good Christian conduct by gender groupings and age. But in Titus 2:7, Paul's words became a personal edict for Titus only. He knew the "worthless" deeds of those causing friction needed to not only stop but would require some visible counteraction as well. So the spiritually savvy old apostle asked his missionary partner to "show yourself to be an example of good deeds." Sound teachings were important, but these young churches also needed an exemplary role model to observe and follow. As per the old adage, "practice what you teach" was exactly what Titus's situation desperately demanded.

Paul understood the importance for those growing in the faith to have solid examples to follow. Therefore, he specifically asked the church in Philippi to look to himself as a role model and put into practice what he taught and lived out while among them.

> Brethren, join in following my example, and observe those who walk according to the pattern you have in us (Phil. 3:17).

> The things you have learned and received and heard and seen in me, practice these things, and the God of peace will be with you (Phil. 4:9).

These verses address the broader concept of Christian conduct but would include the performance of good works, which is our interest in this study. Paul realized that emulating someone who was not present among them was problematic, so he also recommended that they observe those who conform to his practices. Please realize, however, that not all members in a church are suitable as role models. Like Paul, all role models should be staunch imitators of Christ, so we must use the utmost care when choosing someone to emulate (1 Cor. 11:1).

In no uncertain terms, several role models early in my career at NASA held shaping-power over the engineer and leader I became in my career. I longingly desired to emulate their professionalism, technical excellence, work habits, and leadership qualities. I constantly observed how they conducted themselves and occasionally questioned why they chose certain courses of action. Human space flight is a dangerous business and having good role models was paramount in becoming a good rocket scientist.

In a similar fashion, Paul needed Titus to step up to the plate as a role model for the Cretan Christians. By observing Titus's good works, Paul knew the positive impact it would make on their development. As we mentioned earlier, many people like to do their good deeds without anyone noticing, but you cannot be a role model if you don't perform at least some of them where others can take notice. Of course, they are not performed to be noticed by others, but for the benefit of others and ultimately to glorify God.

The Cretan Christians needed to observe how Titus went about accomplishing good deeds on several fronts. How did he uncover the needs of others in the first place? Many people are private about such things. How did he handle delicate situations? Where did he obtain his resources? What skills did he use? When did he illicit help? How did he address others in their time of need? They needed to see his care for others in action. Obviously, many of the good deeds Titus performed could not be seen by all, so he would have to be judicious in who accompanied him. Also, making himself available to the Cretan Christians to provide advice and share his knowledge on the ins-and-outs of performing good deeds would have been extremely important. Paul's challenge to Titus to serve as a role model was simultaneously a daunting request and a flattering tribute.

Not all individuals serve as good role models. You may pick up some undesirable attributes because of following questionable models. One friend, who was fairly capable at figuring out what course of action needed to be followed for a given situation, treated people along the way in an atrocious manner. Questioning him about his behavior on one occasion, he told me that he was just mimicking a more experienced individual. Unfortunately, experience is not the "end all" when seeking a role model. Also remember, even the best of human role models are not perfect, so avoid putting them on a pedestal for at some point, you might become disappointed.

Wired for Good Deeds

You probably have heard and used the old adage: "It is more blessed to give than to receive." Oddly, this timeless expression comes from Jesus via Paul. Specifically, the writers of the Gospels did not include this quote from Jesus, however Paul, in his farewell address to the elders of the Ephesian church, directly credited it to Jesus (Acts 20:35). In his summary statement to the elders, Paul stated that he lived by this teaching from Jesus during his time among them. Through the hard work of supporting his own ministry, he was also able to help the weak. In this example, Paul left them with the moral responsibility that they too "must help the weak."

In the above expression, Jesus is stating that the receiver is definitely blessed in what he receives, but the giver actually benefits more. In recent years, research has actually shown just how blessed the giver truly is. Not only will the giver typically experience greater happiness, but many health benefits can result as well. Improving self-esteem, lowering blood pressure, reducing stress levels, increasing longevity, improving immunity, and reducing chronic pain appear to be associated with performing good works in the lives of others. When you give of yourself to help someone in need, the brain releases the hormone oxytocin, which in turn, reduces your stress. And by way of reward, the brain also releases endorphins to make you feel better, which reinforces your virtuous activity. Similar to "runner's high," this "helper's high" will provide you with a built-in stimulus to carry out more good deeds in the future. You see, God wired you for performing good deeds.[12]

A number of years ago when I was dining with several of my friends and colleagues, the waitress brought the bill to the table, and one of my buddies quickly took the check and said, "I will take care of it." That was not the norm as we always paid for our own meals. We immediately protested and asked him why he wanted to pay for our lunch. He provided his rationale in this short and simple statement, "It will make me happy." Medical research supports that performing such a good deed will probably result in his happiness, but whatever the case, I appreciated his generosity.

To be perfectly clear, I am not suggesting helping others to achieve emotional and physical benefits. You perform good deeds because you care for those in need. As Christians, our giving should never be focused inward, but outward. The blessings we experience from our good deeds is from the masterful work of a giving God, through Whose wisdom we are incentivized to continue helping others.

■ GOOD DEEDS TO PONDER

Sometimes we figure out early in our lives which areas of good works zealously motivate us. For others, major life events may occur later that stir their passions to tend to specific needs. Hopefully, these two good deeds incite a God-directed fervor within you.

A Good Deeds Zealot

When you turn 86, and cannot drive anymore because of macular degeneration and Alzheimer's, you would think that backing off a little would be appropriate. But for one lady, loving God means loving people, and when your 89 year old brother is willing to drive you virtually anywhere, why back off. With a God-given passion to help the underprivileged, she learned a long time ago what she needed to do.

For the last twenty years, this lady has coordinated an army of volunteers from her church to serve the "Lord's Lunch" at the Ocoee Christian Service Center. Every second Saturday, a team of eight adults prepares a couple of entrees, vegetables, and desserts to feed forty needy individuals. No one serves more than once a year, so she coordinates ninety-six workers to pull off this herculean feat throughout the year. There is no paid staff to help or budget support from her church; the volunteers furnish the food and serve, as needed. Every month she decorates the tables at this blessed event and provides the table settings. Not to be left out of the joy of serving at one of these lunches, she participates on the May team.

For this good deeds zealot, not only did she want to pull her church friends into active service, she desired to mobilize her family as well. For the last several years, she and her family have cooked dinner for around 20 men in the Orlando Christian Service Center's Fresh Start Program. These men are in rehabilitation for alcohol and drug abuse and are trying to get back on their feet. Again this benevolent woman and her family prepare and pay for this meal. She has most recently been avidly searching for a replacement act of service because this good program sadly lost their funding.

Her life group also uses her coordination skills by arranging a visit to a local nursing home on the second Sunday of the month to sing old hymns to some of the residents. They try to visit approximately fifteen ladies in their rooms, and many of those like to join in with these a *cappella* joy-givers. At times, this merry chorus will even cut loose cheerfully in song for someone in the hallway.

Hearing comments like "we love you" and "we love that you come" fuels her passions. She loves to know that she is helping someone and believes these activities are God-pleasing. She also serves as a greeter at her church every Sunday, helps with the church's Young at Heart program, and uses her life group to prepare and furnish a meal for the occasional newcomers' luncheon. By the way, in her spare time, she is an avid bridge player. I am sure the other ladies love having this strategic thinker as their partner.

A Heart for Children

You may recall that in 2004, a mother offered emotional appeals on television for the safe return of her daughter, Carlie Brucia. News outlets from across the nation were airing a short video of a man abducting her beloved 11-year-old daughter from a car wash in Sarasota, Florida. Sadly, only a few days passed before this fun-loving little girl's body was found in the woods on the property of Sarasota's Central Church of Christ. Horrified by the abduction, rape, and murder of this innocent child, the community and this church decided to respond to this evil with good. They came together to build the Garden of Joy and Prayer Walk on the church's grounds in the vicinity of where Carly's body was found. Adorned with fountains, a bridge, flowering plants, and comforting words memorialized on stone, this serene setting is a wonderful tribute.

But the Central Church of Christ did not stop there; child safety became one of their core ministries. For eight years on the church's grounds, they hosted a child safety rally on the Saturday before the Super Bowl. More than forty agencies participated with a peak participation of about 1500 concerned visitors from the community. Obviously, an event of this nature required a considerable amount of participation from the church's membership to coordinate, advertise, and prepare the site for the rally.

To further battle the war against child abuse and neglect, Central created an initiative called Believers Against Abuse and Neglect of Kids (BAANK). BAANK attempts to bridge the gap between governmental child welfare agencies and faith-based organizations. The goal is to unify and equip the faith-based community to fight against child abuse and neglect in the most tactful and effectual way possible within governmental constraints.

BAANK oversees a program called Operation Relaxation that provides a night out for foster parents. It's basically a four-hour Vacation Bible School-like event, where the children do crafts, play games, play on the playground, and attend Bible class. Working with local child welfare organizations, churches are certified by requiring background checks and child safety training of their volunteers who will be working with the children.

As a participant in its own program, Central utilizes around thirty-five of its members to host an Operation Relaxation night. As you might expect, sharing in such a good work not only benefits the foster parents and children, but also benefits the volunteers. Involvement in this marvelous work has forever impacted the program's point person. As an individual, she has blossomed in using her God-given talents, skills, and gifts to the fullest, while devoting her life to this noble cause, even becoming a recognized guardian *ad litem* to officially watch out for the welfare of children as a court appointee.

Such programs as BAANK provide an array of opportunities to perform good works. And for two ladies who love crafting, Operation Relaxation provided them the perfect venue to share their gifts. Though one excelled in preparing raw wooden objects beforehand for the children to create their masterpieces, the other wheelchair-bound artist led the children in applying their creative talents to the individual crafts.

Recently I performed a seminar at Central and witnessed a family, who had fostered eighty-five children, place membership at this noble congregation because of the church's capacity to understand the struggles endured by foster families. Through the insights gained from their new ministry, these Christians developed the ability to spiritually nurture an often overlooked group.

Questions

1. When disharmony and factious behavior beset a congregation, how does this impact the performance of good deeds? Why is this the case? What kind of environment do you believe is conducive for performing good deeds?

2. When a Christian's lifestyle is not markedly different from those in the world, what types of detrimental impacts might result from non-Christians who observe such behavior?

3. Paul told Titus in verse 2:14 that Jesus desires for Himself a people "zealous for good deeds." How do you believe this zealousness comes about?

4. Do you feel a zeal for performing any particular types of good

deeds? What specifically are they? Are you following through on this zeal? What might be the problem if you do not have such zeal?

5. How does indifference impact the performance of good deeds?

6. Do you have any role models that provide an excellent example when it comes to performing good deeds? What drew you to them? What specifically do you need to learn from this role model to help you step out a little more in performing good deeds?

7. I would like for you to recall a specific time when you reached out to someone who was in need. Describe how you specifically felt. How were you blessed?

CHAPTER 4

Ever Ready

**And God is able to make all grace abound to you,
that always having all sufficiency in everything,
you may have an abundance for every good deed.**

(2 Cor. 9:8)

The Space Shuttle's launch countdown procedure actually started several days prior to liftoff. And for those of us who participated in this lengthy series of events, "routine" was how we liked to describe this time period. Unexpected busyness meant problems had arisen, and a number of technical issues could easily cause a launch-scrub. Nevertheless, as we came out of the hold at T-minus 9 minutes (T-9M) and the countdown clock started making its way to zero; "routine" became an inappropriate descriptor for the upcoming minutes, no matter how routinely the countdown actually progressed. Adrenaline started pumping and an internal excitement gripped all of us during the Shuttle's last few minutes on her launch pad.

At the Space Shuttle Main Engines (SSME) Avionics console, my colleagues and I anxiously watched our monitors at T-5M, when one of the astronauts started the Auxiliary Power Units (APUs). When up and running, these hydrazine-powered pumps delivered three thousand pounds of hydraulic pressure to a number of systems on the Orbiter, including the three SSMEs. At T-4M, the flight computers issued the Purge Sequence Four command to the three main engines, and on acceptance, the Engine Controllers configured the engines for flight. This included allowing hydraulic pressure to flow to the pistons that opened and closed the SSMEs' servo-actuated valves. At this point, a slight movement in the closed direction could be detected as the hydraulic pressure pushed the valves firmly into their hard-stops, giving us the assurance they were functional and ready for liftoff.

As the Shuttle's liquid hydrogen tank was pressurized for flight at T-1M57S, the last of our measurements shortly came within limits to allow ignition, and the software annunciated "Engine Ready" for each SSME. If the SSMEs were not in the Engine Ready mode, their controllers would reject the Start Enable and Start commands from the flight computers. As long as the engines remained in "Engine Ready," they were in a state of readiness for liftoff. If the commands came, the ignition sequence would begin. Exciting times!

Readiness

Like the majestic SSMEs in Engine Ready, Christians should be poised in a state of readiness to perform good deeds. In fact, Paul asked Titus to jog the memories of the Cretan Christians to exhibit this trait along with several other virtuous characteristics and behaviors he wanted them to live by.

> Remind them to be subject to rulers, to authorities, to be obedient, to be ready for every good deed, to malign no one, to be peaceable, gentle, showing every consideration for all men (Titus 3:1-2).

At first glance, you might quickly jump on board with Paul's teaching, but in rereading the passage you note the word *every*. An unsettling feeling might start to overwhelm you as your mind entertains the thought, *How can I possibly solve all the pressing needs of those around me?* Obviously, Paul knows each individual Christian cannot *solve* "every" need, but you should be willing to jump in and help the best you know how. Perhaps collectively you can help contribute to meeting a need or find someone who knows how to address a particular problem. Sometimes the only thing you might be able to accomplish is pray over and/or spiritually comfort the person.

Readiness has various aspects to it, so what might the Christian's state of readiness to perform good deeds look like?

Compassionate and Opportunistic Eyes

Readiness involves living life with our eyes wide open. As we go about our daily routines, we should be on the lookout for the opportunities God has placed before us to perform good deeds. Often in my past, so much chaos existed in my life that I was like a horse with blinders on. I could only see what was directly in front of me, not around me. Plodding down my own self-directed path, others' needs were blocked from my sight. Nothing but my own concerns could be picked up on my radar screen. On those occasions when I missed an opportunity to come to someone's aid, the following thoughts later haunted my conscience, *How could I have not seen that opportunity to help? I will never get it back.* What a horrible feeling and sad state!

Jesus' eyes took notice of those in need around Him, and we often see in the Bible's stories that His heart was moved by their dilemmas. Matthew recorded the following concerning Jesus:

> Seeing the people, He felt compassion for them, because they were distressed and dispirited like sheep without a shepherd (Matt. 9:36).

Like Jesus, we need to "see" those around us, and I mean really "see" them. We take notice of what they are going through in life, and hopefully our hearts will be moved compassionately by their circumstances. I fairly often have prayed for God to open my eyes to the opportunities before me, but I believe we also need to ask Him to prick our hearts as well. And if you pray that prayer, be ready to act, because you will likely see a boat-load of people to whom you can reach out.

Willingness

Our state of readiness should include an inherent *willingness* to help others. This is not a willingness that comes from the cold letters of some law but one derived from a heart formed in the type of compassion demonstrated by our Savior but is a willingness drenched in the care for others, which calls us into action when life deals them a tough blow or has created a pressing need. On one occasion, a leper desperately sought out Jesus and asked, "Lord, if You are willing, You can make me clean" (Matt. 8:2). The leper's appealing to Jesus' willingness should not be viewed as a lack of faith. To the contrary, the leper faithfully recognized Jesus' authority and power to accomplish such a miraculous healing. Jesus reached out and touched the leper and graciously said, "I am willing; be cleansed" (Matt. 8:3). Only moments earlier this outcast of society probably shamefully announced his presence by shouting out "Unclean, Unclean!" But Jesus' willingness not only led to a miraculous healing of the leprous man, He also gave him the gift of human touch that he probably sorely missed. Jesus could have healed the leper without ever putting His hand on him by means of His powerful words, but the Great Physician compassionately reached out and touched society's untouchable. Jesus did not break the Law by touching what was unclean; He mercifully fulfilled the Law by cleansing the man and, of course, had the power to remain undefiled as well. "I am willing" should be our slogan as we encounter opportunities to perform good deeds.[13]

We must always remember though, that at our conversion, we may not all exhibit the quality of compassion mentioned above. We may know we need to help others (perhaps a rudimentary willingness), but our hearts may not yet be formed in the trait of compassion. For some of us, God's Spirit may have a lot of work to accomplish in our hearts. Nonetheless, the Spirit knows the task at hand and may place a desire in us to help someone in need for the purpose of developing our hearts in the trait of compassion. When we perform good deeds in the lives of others, we give the Spirit something to work with. Seeing the expressive eyes and hearing the appreciative words of those we help reinforces our benevolent behavior and most certainly serves to help form our developing hearts.

Sadly, the enemy of willingness is a heart set on satisfying one's own desires. If you do not feel moved to help others in need, look internally at what is precipitating such an attitude. In all likelihood, your own selfish interests are blocking your willingness to reach out to others. Once you understand that about yourself, you can work on your spiritual life to correct it. Don't worry, our God lives inside of you to help you change, but you first need to be internally confronted by this shortcoming.

A thriving and healthy willingness reminds me of a hound dog that catches the scent of a fox and takes off. You cannot help yourself. When you know someone is in need, you are on the trail of how to satisfy it and will feel no contentment until you contribute somehow. Let's catch that scent!

Presence and Availability

Often, we just need to be present or available to help others. The act of presence opens up many diverse opportunities to reach out to those in need. Can you remember performing a simple good deed just because of your presence, such as opening a door for someone, helping a friend carry a heavy load, or placing something on an upper shelf for a loved one or friend recovering from shoulder surgery? My wife is a physical therapist, and she often talks about the goals she helps patients set while they recover from orthopedic-type surgeries. Past effort-free tasks can become painful and difficult after surgeries, if they can be accomplished at all, so after shoulder surgery, patients may have the simple goal of obtaining a glass from the kitchen cabinet. Until they can achieve that goal, your presence might just allow you to accomplish the thing Jesus asked you to do—give a drink to the thirsty.

When somebody is going through a life crisis, the act of your presence may contribute to her finding some solace. You might need just to hold her and let her cry on your shoulder. Don't try to stop the tears; she needs to release those pent-up emotions. When a close friend has a loved one undergoing a traumatic surgery, you might want to stay with her in the hospital's waiting room. Under the right circumstances, you may want to briefly take hold of her hand to reassure her or gently lay your hand upon her shoulder. Saying a little prayer with her at such a moment might lift up her beleaguered spirits, knowing that you have asked God to intervene on her loved one's behalf. The soothing effect of the human touch is an amazing thing. I remember at my father's funeral a friend who just gently placed his hand on my shoulder. It was all he could do, but his empathy penetrated deeply inside my heart. And at times, we just need to sit quietly and listen to those who are hurting. Let them pour out their soul and sort out their feelings. You might provide some minor insights here and there, but during times of another person's crisis, we typically just need to go into "listen mode."

And when I say *present*, I mean to be present physically, cognitively, and spiritually. You should be totally present with the people to whom you are reaching out. Focus your attention and love on them; the worries of this world will sort themselves out.

Always remember, some people struggle with accepting help. You may need to do more than just say, "Give me a call if you need anything." That is a kind offer but is rarely heeded. It might be best to drop by for a few minutes and truly understand their situation and how one could help.

Presence; it's a wonderful gift!

Courage

Some good deeds may require us to get out of our comfort zones. To carry out those good deeds, we may have to rally a little courage or boldness. Coming face-to-face with the "unknown" often has a way of making us apprehensive. This may be for a good reason, but many times a lack of experience or confidence can make us feel a little uneasy with certain situations. We may need to develop a little courage for several reasons, such as inherent danger, lack of familiarity with an individual, fear of rejection, or fear that you might fail or even make things worse. Your willingness might be present, but your lack of courage can leave you in a quandary. And from my experience, we often do not know how we will react until we are faced with a particular set of circumstances.

According to Mark's account of the events surrounding the cross, courage did not appear to come easily to Joseph of Arimathea when he contemplated going to Pilate to ask for Jesus' body after His death.

> When evening had already come, because it was the preparation day, that is, the day before the Sabbath, Joseph of Arimathea came, a prominent member of the Council, who himself was waiting for the kingdom of God; and he gathered up courage and went in before Pilate, and asked for the body of Jesus (Mark 15:42-43).

Jesus was crucified around 9 a.m. in the morning (Mark 15:25) and died around 3 p.m. (Mark 15:34), but Joseph did not ask Pilate for Jesus' body until that evening (between 4 p.m. and 5 p.m.). John recorded in his Gospel that Joseph was a "secret" disciple of Jesus "for fear of the Jews" (Jn. 19:38). Being connected to Jesus could be costly on several fronts for this respected Jewish leader. Like for many of us, there comes a point when Jesus becomes worth the costs, and for Joseph that time had arrived, so he "gathered up" the courage to seek Pilate out and make his request. By overcoming his fears, Joseph accomplished a good and historic work by taking care of Jesus' burial.[14]

Fear often stands in our way of accomplishing many good deeds, so we need to think through how to remove or mitigate the fears that typically hold us back. Sometimes we just need to overcome our fears by trusting God. Our desire to control everything can displace our ability to trust in His guidance and seek help from Him. Turning to God in prayer, either real-time or at a time we set aside, should be foundational to our approach in helping others and overcoming our fears. Mentoring by others and developing the necessary skills to assist those who face particular issues (such as alcoholism) will instill confidence and help displace our fears. In situations where we may be concerned for our safety, it may be necessary to involve others to assist us. A friend recently shared with me a good work that two elders were undertaking, and they felt it was prudent to bring in the authorities to help address a potentially dangerous situation. In some risky circumstances, our readiness may simply involve bringing in the proper individuals who can address a particular situation in a safe manner.

My friend, David Ford, in his book, *Confessions of a Small Town Minister*, reminded me of something important when it comes to courage and fear. He said, "...that courage is not the absence of fear, but rather courage is the resolve to face whatever is fearful."[15] So let's not allow fear to freeze us in our tracks, but holdfast to what helps us rally the courage to press forward with our good deeds.

Resources

Most of us have more resources available to carry out good deeds than we might imagine. We can use our cars to drive a friend who is recovering from an injury or surgery to the doctor. Our homes can become a safe-haven for others to discuss their problems or a place where hospitality is extended to a family who is new to the area. Time and physical strength become assets to help others perform laborious tasks that are beyond their means, such as clearing brush from a piece of property, cleaning someone's kitchen, or assisting in unloading a moving van. Our churches can often provide us with material to perform Bible studies, as well as funds to help someone make it through financially rough times. And I am sure you can add many more possible resources that might be at our disposal.

Our personal financial resources can also open many doors to accomplish an array of good works. After telling the Christians in Ephesus to be "renewed in the spirit of your mind" and to "put on the new self" (Eph. 4:23-24), Paul offered several examples of the type of holy behavior that should result from their new life orientation; one involved their money (or material resources).

> He who steals must steal no longer; but rather he must labor, performing with his own hands what is good, so that he will have something to share with one who has need (Eph. 4:28).

Paul specifically stated that one of the primary goals of working was to "share with one who has need." Have you ever been taught that? We live in a world that touts prosperity. Does not the American dream consist of nice homes, ritzy cars, current fashions, big retirement savings, and the like? Do we carve out any of our prosperity to help those in need, or is it an afterthought? Have you ever suggested to your children to keep in mind their ability to help others when selecting a career? We have a lot to learn here.

What good deeds could you become involved with if you had the discipline or ability to set aside some money to help others? Here are a few examples to stimulate your thinking; we can help a teen who cannot afford it go to Bible camp, provide food for the hungry, give to those impacted by natural disasters, share a meal with someone who needs advice, or go on a mission trip. Greed can certainly blind us to such opportunities, so you may need to spiritually evaluate your internal attitudes concerning giving. At times, we may simply not be engaged with our churches, causing us to miss out on opportunities to give or help with many gracious works. One thing I am not suggesting though, is that you throw money at good works and never become personally involved. The nature of some good works may just require us to contribute money to a particular cause, but at some point we need to directly serve others in need. Giving money to good causes can be spiritually developmental but directly serving others has much greater formational power.

Planning

Many good deeds spontaneously take place, such as picking up an item someone has dropped. Consequently, they just occur randomly. However, many good works have some level of predictability allowing for us to perform some advance planning prior to undertaking them. If you were a nurse going on a medical mission trip, you might look into the medical issues facing a particular geographical area and bring the appropriate supplies to treat your projected patients. You might service your chainsaw and replace its chain if you decided to go into an area devastated by a hurricane. Inadequate planning is a surefire way to fall short of your goals when attempting many good works. Benjamin Franklin is often attributed as saying, "If you fail to plan, you are planning to fail." Plan to best use your talents and resources when you can.

A couple of years ago, a church asked me to teach the adult portion of their VBS and wanted me to present the talk I give on Spirituality & Spaceflight the first night. Since a "rocket scientist" was going to be in their midst, they decided to develop a space theme for their entire VBS. They built rockets (one had exhaust coming out of its nozzles), space shuttles, facades of KSC facilities, and starry night entryways, as well as piped in launch countdown audio. Their creation served as backdrops for space-themed skits that illustrated biblical concepts. Such extensive planning and effort resulted in a bunch of starry-eyed children who immersed themselves in the experience—a VBS that will be remembered for years to come.

I could mention several other examples, but let's direct our thinking into a couple of particular areas. If you know someone who needs encouraging or has done something worthy of praise, put some forethought into the specific words you might use to build them up the next time you see them. Spontaneity may still rule the conversation, but by anticipating some of your words, your exchange with them will likely be more productive. By taking notice of them and making a thoughtful comment, even if you consider it a little thing, it may mean the world to them. Never sell short what may result from saying an encouraging word. Encouragement has contributed to changing or guiding my life's course on several occasions.

Some situations may call for spending a little alone time with someone to help him work through an issue or to encourage him to press on to new heights in his walk with God. Think about how you might come alongside and spend a little time with someone if he will allow it. One thing that has worked for me on several occasions is to ask the individual to go to an out-of-town restaurant with me. Unless he talks to me about something, the night is going to be fairly boring and awkward, since we will be spending quite a bit of time together in the car and restaurant. At some point, the conversation tends to allow itself to go in a direction where you can constructively help that person out or build him up. Whatever you do, respect where he takes the conversation, and afterward, his confidentiality.

God's Word

Nothing will prepare us for accomplishing good deeds like God's Word. Thoroughly studying the Bible allows us to understand God's will for serving others and provides the spiritual under-pinnings for properly taking on all good works. Paul shared with Timothy the critical connection of inspired Scripture and carrying out good works.

> All Scripture is inspired by God and profitable for teaching, for reproof, for correction, for training in righteousness; that the man of God may be adequate, equipped for every good work (2 Tim. 3:16-17).

In the past, I have noted that some teachers place an emphasis on verse sixteen and treat seventeen as an afterthought. They use verse sixteen as their grounds to zealously attack others' beliefs in an effort to prove them wrong. Unfortunately, they missed the primary point of Paul's rich teaching. Inspired Scripture's purpose is to prepare us "for every good work." The teaching, reproof, correction and training in righteousness acquired from God's Word serves to equip us to come to the aid of those with physical and spiritual needs which would include sharing the gospel message.

In the next chapter, we will look at how the Bible prepares us spiritually to carry out good deeds. But let's look at another effective way that God's Word prepares us for our works of goodness. God has shared with us many stories to illustrate when and how to go about performing good deeds. These narratives help us develop compassionate hearts that are moved by the dilemmas of others as well as instilling a servant mindset. They include such stories as the parable of The Good Samaritan, the washing of apostles' feet, the feeding of the masses, and the many stories of healings.

In a discussion of the Judgment in Matt. 25:31-46, Jesus shared that when someone addressed the needs of His "brothers, even the least of them" (Matt. 25:40) that it was equivalent to directly performing these works of compassion for Him. Please wrap your hearts and minds around Jesus' words—helping a brother in need is like helping Him. A remarkable teaching to say the least! Notice the particular good deeds Jesus brought to light.

> For I was hungry, and you gave Me *something* to eat; I was thirsty, and you gave Me *something* to drink; I was a stranger, and you invited Me in; naked, and you clothed Me; I was sick, and you visited Me; I was in prison, and you came to Me (Matt. 25:35-36).

Per Jesus, the righteous are identified by such good deeds, and they are the ones who will enter "into eternal life" (Matt. 25:46).

D. A. Carson sums up Jesus' words this way:

> Good deeds done to Jesus' followers, even the least of them, are not only works of compassion and morality but reflect where people stand in relation to the kingdom and to Jesus Himself.[16]

Get into the Word folks, and prepare your minds and hearts for carrying out good deeds—it has eternal ramifications.

Special Training and Mentoring

I would like to end our exploration of the Christian's state of readiness to perform good works by briefly mentioning two additional items. First, have you ever considered taking any specific training to facilitate your ability to help meet the needs of others? Educating yourself in a particular ministry activity or trade should open many doors for you to help others. Let's look at a couple of examples to stimulate your thinking. Perhaps you're stirred internally to contribute more than money to build housing for the poor. If so, you might consider taking some coursework in construction management. Such training will give you the knowledge to build homes that are cost-effective, safe and that last, as well as giving you a foundation in the national and local codes for residential construction projects.

From a ministry perspective, you might want to consider counseling. I have some good friends who credit the advice of a counselor as being instrumental in saving their marriage. Years ago, a counselor re-instilled in me a confidence I had lost because of some difficult life circumstances that I had experienced. By the way, all counselors are not created equal, at least as far as their advice goes. Some have troubling values, biases, and orientations that guide their advice. I remember a friend whose wife was receiving counseling and was given guidance that I felt was unethical. As my friend's wife had fallen short of some particular life goals, the counselor told her that she needed to continue to try to achieve them at all costs, even at the expense of her marriage and children. Selfish ambitions were first in this counselor's mind. The counselor's concern for her patient's loved ones and reconciliation were disregarded. This counselor had some deeply perverted values. Our nation needs good counselors who advise others from a solid Christian ethic and understand our spiritual side.

Receiving mentoring in an area of interest to us is another good way to effectively prepare ourselves for specific good works. In the last chapter, we discussed the value of a good role model, but in the case of a mentor, we are talking about a deeper relationship to another person and commitment to learning. Paul's relationship to Titus was as mentor to apprentice. Titus learned from Paul how to plant churches, nurture them, share the gospel message, deal with conflict, as well as many other things. A mentor's role is to pass on practical knowledge and help one develop the specific skills necessary to competently undertake work in a targeted area. As I mentioned earlier, a good mentor instills confidence within his apprentice.

You might want to participate in mission work but do not feel you are particularly gifted at evangelism. Nevertheless, you still deeply believe in it and want to somehow facilitate it. After learning that some missionaries need the help of well-drillers to provide clean water for those they are trying to evangelize, you realize that this might be right down your alley because of your mechanical skills, but you lack familiarity with drilling for water. In such a case, you could potentially find a mentor in the drilling trade to prepare you for the mission field.

By the way, mentoring is a two-way street. Not only should you have the desire for a particular individual to mentor you, but your mentor, in turn, needs to possess the desire to provide you with the mentoring. She may have a valid reason to reject your request; respect it and press on to find another one. A flawed mentoring relationship may cause you to lose your zeal for a particular area of work. Hopefully at some point, you will create a wealth of practical knowledge you, too, can pass on as a mentor to a future good deed doer in God's kingdom.

The Consummate Good Deed

I doubt any good deed story in the Bible stands out more in the modern mind than the parable of the Good Samaritan. It serves as an excellent example of the various aspects of good deed readiness we have been discussing. Jesus shared this parable while in a discussion with an expert of the Jewish Law over what one must do to "inherit eternal life."

> And a lawyer stood up and put Him to the test, saying, "Teacher, what shall I do to inherit eternal life?" And He said to him, "What is written in the Law? How does it read to you?" And he answered, "YOU SHALL LOVE THE LORD YOUR GOD WITH ALL YOUR HEART, AND WITH ALL YOUR SOUL, AND WITH ALL YOUR STRENGTH, AND WITH ALL YOUR MIND; AND YOUR NEIGHBOR AS YOURSELF." And He said to him, "You have answered correctly; DO THIS AND YOU WILL LIVE." But wishing to justify himself, he said to Jesus, "And who is my neighbor?" Jesus replied and said, "A man was going down from Jerusalem to Jericho, and fell among robbers, and they stripped him and beat him, and went off leaving him half dead. And by chance a priest was going down on that road, and when he saw him, he passed by on the other side. Likewise a Levite also, when he came to the place and saw him, passed by on the other side. But a Samaritan, who was on a journey, came upon him; and when he saw him, he felt compassion, and came to him and bandaged up his wounds, pouring oil and wine on *them*; and he put him on his own beast, and brought him to an inn and took care of him. On the next day he took out two denarii and gave them to the innkeeper and said, 'Take care of him; and whatever more you spend, when I return I will repay you.' Which of these three do you think proved to be a neighbor to the man who fell into the robbers' *hands?*" And he said, "The one who showed mercy toward him." Then Jesus said to him, "Go and do the same" (Lk. 10:25-37).

When the lawyer queried Jesus as to "who is my neighbor," Jesus recognized the restrictive tone of the question. The lawyer's concern dealt with who fell within that inner circle that he must love, rather than what being a loving neighbor looks like. So Jesus answered his question by sharing the story of The Good Samaritan, but also has the lawyer examine another pertinent question—"What behaviors does a loving neighbor exhibit?"[17] Like the lawyer, do you ever find yourself wanting to limit to whom you extend your love?

So what aspects of readiness to perform good deeds are exhibited by the Good Samaritan in this parable? Several are demonstrated, but none hold the significance like the state of the Samaritan's heart, as the whole story turned on his compassion. He "saw" and he "felt compassion." Jesus mentioned no words concerning the hearts of the priest and the Levite, because their lack of action portrayed that their hearts were devoid of mercy. All three "saw" the plight of the injured man, but only one looked on with compassion in his heart. All three "knew" what to do, but only a heart prepared in the trait of compassion had the steering power necessary to propel the Samaritan in the appropriate direction.

Jesus next addressed the willingness of each to be a neighbor. He stated that the priest and Levite "passed by on the other side" of the road. Jesus' vivid depiction of these "unwilling" two highlighted just how *un*loving they were. They could not get far enough away from the beaten man, as they sought to avoid him; not too neighborly. Before being too critical, have you ever given someone in need a wide berth as you made your way by him? Jesus then succinctly stated that the Good Samaritan "came to him." No hesitancy was mentioned; his compassion guided his actions. The lawyer by now was horrified as Jesus revealed that "a neighbor" was not defined by nationality, race, or religion. The supposed "righteous" priest and Levite left someone in desperate need of help to die by the roadside, while the "despised" Samaritan came to his rescue. We could speculate as to why the priest and Levite did not help, but in actuality, it is totally irrelevant. Jesus' point was that they were *unwilling* to come to the man's aid, while the Samaritan was *willing*. The beaten man needed a neighbor, and only the Samaritan stepped up to this desperately needed calling.

In coming to the aid of the injured man, the Good Samaritan exhibited great courage. Jesus assuredly picked this road for His story because of its well-known dangers. Robbers took advantage of the rough terrain that lined this lonely stretch of road to ambush hapless passersby. As the Samaritan approached the beaten man, the robbers could possibly have been lurking behind an outcropping of rocks or in a cave waiting for him to stop and lend a hand, or the whole episode might have been a treacherous ruse to lure in an unsuspecting victim. The Good Samaritan's compassionate heart rallied the courage he needed to take on the risk of coming to this man's aid. Surely you are acquainted with a perilous road or two and understand the type of danger the Samaritan faced.

The thoughtful planning by the kind-hearted Samaritan served him well. The supplies he brought along were not targeted for a specific good deed, but they facilitated his ability to help address the man's wounds. Recently, my wife and I went on a hike at Table Rock State Park in South Carolina. The sky looked rather gray and ominous when we arrived, so she remembered that she had put a couple of inexpensive ponchos in the glove compartment a while back, remnants of the days when we watched our children participate in their outdoor sports. Thankfully, she threw them in our backpack, as her thoughtfulness kept us from getting soaked to the bone during the hike. Good planners can be a godsend.

In this parable though, Jesus was not emphasizing the Samaritan's planning skills, but his willingness to use his resources to help the injured man. The Samaritan's lovingkindness was immediately demonstrated by wisely using his limited resources to care for the man. Turning to the medicines of his day, the Samaritan treated the man's wounds with oil and wine, while bandaging him up. Understanding the serious condition of the man, the Samaritan put aside his own desires and comforts and placed the man on his own animal and led him to a local inn. This provided an environment where he could rest and start recovering from his wounds, while receiving more thorough care. Needing to continue to his original destination on the next day, the Samaritan knew the man in his care had just been robbed and was penniless. So he provided the innkeeper with what equated to about two days' wages to continue to care for the man. He also promised to return and pay any additional costs the innkeeper might incur while attending to the injured man's needs.

Jesus outlined in the parable of The Good Samaritan how "a neighbor" loves on someone in great need. That need should move us to act mercifully in another person's regard while personally sacrificing our own comfort, time, and resources if the situation calls for it. Even the jaded Jewish lawyer could not help but come to the right conclusion. A true neighbor is defined by his compassionate behavior, not by one's nationality, religion, race, economic status, education, or the like. Nothing has changed. Jesus' direction to the lawyer still rings true for us today—"Go" and be a neighbor!

■ GOOD DEEDS TO PONDER
Knowing how best to help others might require us to think over the circumstances for an extended period of time, while in other cases a cry for help will spontaneously propel us into action. Each individual's situation will produce different demands as to how we should move forward to accomplish the good deed.

Tool-Time

Week after week during his congregation's announcements, Scott listened to the heartrending reports of Larry's fight for survival (true story but names have been changed). He did not know this father-of-three well, but sitting idly by was no longer an option for him. In and out of hospitals for months on end, Larry's condition was becoming critical as he was in desperate need of a kidney transplant. Unfortunately, a weak heart was holding him back from being a viable candidate for this precious organ transplant. The doctors were trying to increase his heart's efficiency through medication, but complications kept progress at a nerve-racking slow pace.

Deciding to show their support, Scott and his wife started to visit Larry in the hospital, while also trying to comfort Larry's wife, Lisa, as well. The lengthy hospital stays and surgeries had depleted the family's finances and had thrust Lisa into several new family roles, placing her under a tremendous amount of stress. Driving almost an hour from their home to the hospital everyday was a real burden, especially in a mini-van that had seen better days. And on one occasion during Scott's visit, Lisa asked for his advice concerning an issue with the brakes on the van. Being mechanically gifted, Scott volunteered to look at it under her protest. Sadly, he discovered rather quickly that she needed a part that cost two thousand dollars. However, this resourceful man found a van of the same model in a nearby junkyard and procured the part for fifty dollars. So after installing it and changing her oil, she had a vehicle with a proper functioning brake system again.

Not long after this, Larry's father passed away, and the family needed to drive about eight hundred miles to attend the funeral and spend time with relatives. But the old family van was in no condition to make such a trip. Lisa had a local automotive repair shop address a serious oil leak from the van's engine, but even after repairs, this vital lubricating fluid kept oozing out of the engine to such an extent that she kept a bottle of oil with her at all times to occasionally add some when necessary. Stepping up in this time of need, one of the members of their church graciously loaned them a car, so they went to the funeral in a safe and reliable vehicle.

While they were gone, Scott wanted to investigate why the engine was leaking so much oil. The family could not afford a new vehicle at this point or a major repair bill, so perhaps there was something he could do. Scott's father had a garage with a lift, so he took the van there to assess the problem. He could hardly believe his eyes as the oil was leaking out from all over the engine. He knew what now faced him to keep this family in a safe running vehicle; the engine needed to be removed and torn down. Scott had never pulled an engine from a minivan before, and he only had a week to take on this extensive endeavor. And he could not take time off from his work, so to finish this job in a week would require several challenging nights and a weekend of hard work. Nevertheless, Scott had grown to love this family, so with the help of his father and a couple of Christian brothers, they proceeded to pull and tear down the engine. Once apart, they cleaned all the parts, ordered replacements where needed, and replaced all the engine's seals. Some parts were not available locally and were ordered online via two-day mail. Members from his church came up with the money to cover the cost of the parts. To keep them on task, Scott's wife pitched in by delivering food to facilitate their efforts. It was an onerous project, but Scott and his crew completed the task prior to the family's return.

Scott sat down with Larry and Lisa after their arrival and shared with them the list of all the work they had accomplished on the van. Shock quickly overtook them as their jaws dropped in an expression of disbelief. Because of their astonishment, Scott had to tell them twice that they had removed the engine, as he eagerly shared pictures of the engine in its various stages of repair. God stirred the heart of this mechanically gifted man, and he knew the need was great. So he acted. He wanted Larry and Lisa to know that they were family, and he was in it for the long haul with them. For Scott, to accomplish this good deed it meant "Tool Time."

Undaunted Courage—Teenage Style

Steven Conway, a senior at the Mount Dora Christian Academy, demonstrated true sacrifice by saving a victim from her attempted murderer. In April 2015, Steven and Orange Avenue Church of Christ Youth Minister Scott Simpson went to get a drink in a Dollar General store in Eustis after the evening Bible Study. While in the store they heard a woman scream. Steven's immediate response was to intervene. "It was hard to describe," he said. "It was more like a shriek, and I knew she needed help." Without hesitation, he ran toward the commotion and pulled the attacker off of the female clerk. It wasn't until then that Steven realized that it was more than an argument. He saw blood and a butterfly-style knife still lodged in the woman's chest. She had also been slashed in the face and was subsequently airlifted to an Orlando hospital where she recovered. The perpetrator was immediately arrested outside of the store by police, who informed Steven that the attacker had in his possession two

Samurai swords, each more than two feet in length.

Police hailed Steven as a hero, but the senior was modest about his valor, saying he just assisted someone who needed help. His meek demeanor is typical of this young man's character. Steven has attended the Orange Avenue Church of Christ this past school year and was baptized shortly before the incident. He has been a leader and role model in the Class of 2015 and was elected by his classmates as the senior boy with the most school spirit. The secondary faculty and students celebrated Steven's heroics after showing a news broadcast of the incident after chapel. "We are so proud of the selflessness of this young man," says Dr. James Moore (the school's President). "He acted on instinct which, for him, meant thinking of someone else before himself." [This article appeared in the Spring 2015 issue of *Imagine* magazine produced by the school and was used by permission with only minor changes made for the purpose of clarification.]

Questions

1. Christians should be in a state of readiness to perform good deeds. List the aspects of readiness that we should possess or exhibit. Please list any others that you believe are not mentioned in the book.

2. What do you believe are the three most important aspects of readiness? Why? Of those three, on a scale of 1 to 10, how proficient are you at each of them? How might you improve in these areas?

3. What is the foremost reason that would keep you from helping someone in need? Why do you think that is the case?

4. Describe the concept of "presence." Is that hard for you to do? Can you name an instance when Jesus exhibited this quality?

Can you remember a time when someone was present or available for you?

5. Are there certain aspects of performing good deeds that are a little fearful for you? Why do you think that is the case? How might you lessen those fears?

6. How has God's Word prepared you for accomplishing good deeds?

7. If you had the ability, to which good works would you charitably give or give more? Along with giving monetarily, why is it important to serve others as well?

8. What aspects of good deeds readiness did the Good Samaritan exhibit?

CHAPTER 5

Engaging

**...so that you will walk in a manner worthy of the Lord,
to please Him in all respects, bearing fruit in every good work
and increasing in the knowledge of God.**

(Col. 1:10)

E ach Space Shuttle Orbiter possessed a little known capability included in its design and was routinely tested at the Kennedy Space Center. In the cockpit, there were two hand controllers called the Speedbrake/Thrust Controllers (SBTC), one each for the Commander and Pilot. Only the Pilot's SBTC was configured to work as a Thrust Controller. If the Pilot ever depressed the takeover button on the SBTC during powered flight, the flight computers would freeze the thrust level of the three Space Shuttle Main Engines (SSMEs). The Pilot then could move the controller to match the SSMEs current thrust level while keeping the takeover button depressed. Once attaining a match, the Pilot released the button to engage the SBTC, and he then could control the thrust level of the SSMEs via the hand controller.

So how would you like to throttle a vehicle that delivers more than one million pounds of thrust? If your imagination is not racing a little with that thought, please check your pulse. Seriously though, this would be a highly risky maneuver and was designed for use only in extreme abort scenarios. Fortunately, our courageous astronauts never had to use this capability in an actual mission.

Seeing someone struggling with an issue in his life is usually what drives us into action to perform a good deed. During such times, we need to come alongside that person to help. We should not come in all high and mighty like we have all the answers, nor should we take our burdens into his life. Much like the Thrust Controller, we need to try to match that friend's "speed" before we engage. Enter his world and experience his concerns, ills, or grief. We must try to walk in his shoes, as the old saying goes, as you reach out to him to help.

Before engaging in good deeds, Paul has an important reminder to us all concerning this gracious activity.

Saved by Grace, Not Works

So far in Paul's letter to Titus, we have noted that Jesus' sacrifice allowed for the creation of a people that were His own, "zealous for good deeds" (2:14). As such, Paul encouraged the Cretan Christians to be "ready for every good deed" (3:1), and that Titus should serve as "an example of good deeds" (2:7) from which they could learn. Prior to asking the churches to press on with engaging in good works, Paul wanted to make sure they understood the basis of their salvation as it related to their good deeds. Humans tend to want to earn their own way in life, so Paul knew he needed to be perfectly clear with these fledgling believers.

> But when the kindness of God our Savior and *His* love for mankind appeared, He saved us, not on the basis of deeds which we have done in righteousness, but according to His mercy, by the washing of regeneration and renewing by the Holy Spirit, whom He poured out upon us richly through Jesus Christ our Savior, so that being justified by His grace we might be made heirs according to *the* hope of eternal life (Titus 3:4-7).

When it comes to our salvation, it is all about God's grace. The only earning that was accomplished took place on the cross. Our good deeds should be a natural result of what we have become in Christ Jesus. As precious as those deeds are to God, they in no way earn our salvation. Because of Paul's succinctness and clarity to the church in Ephesus, I use the following verse a second time.

> For by grace you have been saved through faith; and that not of yourselves, *it is* the gift of God; not as a result of works, so that no one may boast (Eph. 2:8-9).

Gift, yes a precious gift!

Believers Engage

After providing the churches in Crete with an eloquent theological foundation for their salvation in Titus 3:4-7, Paul proceeded to directly connect God's saving activity to the practical component of Christian living.

> This is a trustworthy statement; and concerning these things I want you to speak confidently, so that those who have believed God may be careful to engage in good deeds. These things are good and profitable for men (Titus 3:8).

In conjunction with the previous verses, Paul wanted them to thoroughly understand that even though performing good deeds may not save them, those who place their trust in God "engage" in them. A proper understanding of God's plan of salvation yields the proper Christian behavior—*engaging* in good deeds. The Christian life is not about sitting on the sidelines and watching God go to work. To follow God is to produce positive visible results in the lives of others. *Good* works performed in love naturally profess that we truly know God, unlike the deeds of the false teachers as mentioned in Titus 1:16.

The Greek word translated above as "careful" has the connotation of giving "sustained thought" to something. So Paul was asking the Cretan churches to give thoughtful consideration in carrying out their Christian purpose and engage in good deeds. The word "engage" in the Greek is also not an insignificant term. It suggests something we take interest in, have care for, and give our devotion to. Carefully considering the needs of others should result in a genuine concern for their well-being and drive us into action. As when one gear engages with another, they become linked together while the one devotedly transfers energy to turn the other. When we engage, let's engage with thoughtfulness and devotion, ready to transfer our energy to directly help the one in need.[18]

Like with a yellow highlighter, Paul constructed a simple

sentence at the end of verse eight to draw his readers' attention to the result of engaging in good deeds; "These things are good and profitable for men." By performing such deeds everyone benefits. The recipients' needs are addressed. Observers gain by the positive example of a good role model. Non-believers see the goodness of God at work through His people, hopefully attracting the recipients (and others) to the Gospel message. Those who conduct the good deeds benefit spiritually, as well as physically and emotionally as we discussed in Chapter 3. Such behavior is profitable to all. Paul reiterates this point as he closed out his letter to Titus.

> Our people must also learn to engage in good deeds to meet pressing needs, so that they will not be unfruitful (Titus 3:14).

Producing good fruit, that is the Christian vocation. Christians performing good deeds help create an environment for the fruit to ripen into wholesome, vitalizing goodness. In contrast, Paul warns against causing strife and exhibiting factious behavior that it is "unprofitable and worthless" (Titus 3:9-11). Such actions are toxic to the fruit and turn it rancid. You probably have seen this type of fruit and smelled its foul stench. Let's give our lives to produce orchards of goodness with the sweet smelling aroma of its ripened fruit.

Urgent Needs

You may have noted that Paul repeated the exact phrase from Titus 3:8 in 3:14, "to engage in good deeds." Obviously, this was not coincidental. He desired to drive home this important theme of his letter as he brought it to a close. But in verse 14, Paul qualified the target of the good deeds—those with "pressing needs." All needs do not require us to go at breakneck speed to address them, but some may have a level of urgency that requires immediate attention.

Back when our daughter was a toddler, she came up to my wife one quiet morning with an alarmed look on her face and started pointing at her nose. While playing quietly for some time, she came across a button. For some strange reason, her naïve little mind had an intriguing thought, *I wonder if this button will fit in my nose?* Low and behold, it did. So as my wife started investigating our daughter's nasal distress, she found a small button wedged deeply back in one of her nostrils. Life suddenly became interrupted by a *pressing* need. A stain on one of our daughter's cute little dresses, a mess in her room, or a broken toy in need of repair all could wait. Urgency suddenly entered our household. We thought about trying to retrieve the button ourselves but were too afraid that we may cause her to ingest it or something worse. So off to the emergency room we went. After strapping her down to keep her perfectly still, the doctor successfully retrieved the button with a long, slender pair of tweezers. After that traumatic adventure, we were ready to get back to the more mundane occurrences of family life.

Paul was not saying in Titus 3:14 that Christians should only do good deeds related to pressing matters. He already stated that we need to stand ready "for every good deed." However, *true* "pressing needs" deserve special emphasis. As you well know, some people can create a personal crisis that is not pressing. Many needs, however, are unquestionably urgent, such as medical emergencies, death of a loved one, devastation from natural disasters, a family with no food or basic necessities, and the like. We should be ever-vigilant and ready to minister to others in such circumstances. That is what Christians do!

Knowledge not from Books

You might ask, "How do I find out about the needs of others? I want to help out when possible." Some needs might get identified during announcements at our churches, noted in our congregations' bulletins, or made known on some social media outlet.

Typically though, these mostly take the form of prayer requests. We need to honor those of course, but what about those needs that require us to reach out to someone and directly help? How do we find out about those needs? Many organizations exist for the sole purpose of carrying out good deeds of some sort and may provide you with the opportunity to directly serve others, such as food banks, soup kitchens, homeless shelters, and homes for children. In such organizations, people in need tend to make their way to them and provide an institutionalized capability to engage in good deeds. But what about our daily relationships, is there a way to help surface the needs of people who walk in our circles? Often, many people are too proud to publicly announce their needs. Some folks do not want to burden others with their problems. Many needs may also be of a private nature. Some people may not want others coming to their home because it is unkempt, and you probably can come up with some additional reasons as well. So again, how do we uncover these needs?

We should never expect others to reveal their needs unless we truly come to "know" them. Due to past experiences, some people have been conditioned to be untrusting. They will not make themselves vulnerable by revealing certain things about their lives such as their personal needs. Do not expect a trusting relationship with someone to develop overnight, they often take years to develop. Some people might be prone to trust a minister or elder because of their position or office, but even in those cases, the person in need has probably observed how they ministered to others in the past.

Building relationships is a personal investment in others. They learn what we believe, and whether our actions are consistent with what we profess. They come to understand whether we care about them or are selfishly motivated. They make a determination whether we can be trusted with their personal information, and if we have the ability to potentially help them. I'll never forget one particular Sunday morning a number of years ago; I was talking with one my Christian brothers in the foyer of our auditorium before services began. From the corner of my eye, I suddenly saw one of my close friends open the backdoor of the foyer and make a beeline straight for me. As he approached, I noticed he looked disheveled and horribly upset. He immediately pulled me aside and revealed a shocking problem that was consuming him. Ministry was not going to take place that morning by going into the auditorium and listening to a sermon. After just a few minutes, I knew what I needed to do, so I drove him to a local park, where we could talk in private. He poured his soul out to me for the next hour while crying uncontrollably. Knowing this man like I did, there was no way he would have shared the intimate details of his issue without a deep trust in me. That trust developed over a long period of time, and even then, it took utter desperation for him to reach out to me. It just was not in his make-up to lean on others.

In a culture where fences isolate us from our neighbors, our "friends" reside in social media, and texting often replaces actually talking with one another, the art of growing relationships is a lot harder. When I was growing up, some of our neighbors were in and out of our house throughout the day. People can share intimate conversations over a cup of coffee or a cordial lunch. With no fences around our adjacent neighbors' homes, I often saw conversations start up for the simple reason that my parents saw their friends working outside in the yard or relaxing on a back porch. Some of these families grew quite close. I remember when my dad was breathing laboriously during the last minutes of his life, and a long-term, caring neighbor came over to hold his hand and support him as my father passed from this world. At the time, I was surprised and thought his presence and actions were an extremely difficult thing for him, but because of a warm relationship with my father that had evolved through the years, it enabled him to enter this sacred space at my father's death.

Social media and texting have their place but for relationships to truly develop, we need to look into our friends' eyes. We need to hear the tone of their voice, see their facial expressions, and observe their body language. Such insights help us understand what they are thinking, and how to direct our conversations and actions.

Going regularly to a church can aid us in building relationships. Just attending worship services can serve us in an introductory way to become acquainted with others, but we need to allow time before and after services to talk and mingle with others a little. Attending fellowships will also facilitate getting to know others, as conversations often go to the next level at such events. Small groups or in-home Bible studies tend to help relationships flourish. Such smaller gatherings typically promote camaraderie, and people begin to become a little more relaxed and open up as trust develops. I preached and taught at a house church for a number of years as well as led small groups in the past, and I can personally attest that the bonds of fellowship and love can run deep among the members of these gatherings. Tears and laughter easily flowed in these groups because of the close bonds that developed, and pressing needs were much easier to identify.

Deep friendships can also evolve when we work on special activities together at our churches, such as when you work with a handful of devoted individuals on a mission trip, at a work camp, on a fellowship initiative, or for Vacation Bible School.

Any of the above has the potential to open up a relationship that will continue to grow outside the church's "four walls." These relationships might include some of the following: sharing meals, playing sports, working on hobbies, serving others, or just enjoying one another's company. Whatever works for both of you, just get to "know" one another. Hopefully, the type of bonds will develop that allow for the sharing of pressing needs when they arise, and they will arise.

I am not suggesting that we restrict our relationships to our churches. That is just a good starting place. In fact, building relationships with others in our communities is extremely important if we want to have an influence on the world for Christ. We also need to realize that some people are hard to get close to or may not have the desire to take a relationship much deeper than a superficial level for a number of reasons. Do not be offended; instead respect it. You never know how things may work out later.

If we want to be involved with others, we have to break down the walls that tend to isolate us in our culture. The end result is to make meaningful connections with others and to truly come to "know" them. Develop deep enough relationships where they can confide in us, so we can come to them at their time of need and engage in a good deed. If we cannot personally help them, at least we know of their issues so we can pray for them and possibly attain help for them, if they are willing.

Engaging Qualities

Our spirituality plays a crucial role when we engage in good deeds. One's inner attitudes and character traits not only move us to reach out to others but regulate our behaviors while performing a good work. Our inner-being will continue to develop throughout our lives, but we should start carrying out good deeds even in our infancy as Christians. Nevertheless, some works are best left for the spiritually mature. Paul identified such a case to the church in Galatia.

> Brethren, even if anyone is caught in any trespass, you who are spiritual, restore such a one in a spirit of gentleness; each one looking to yourself, so that you too will not be tempted (Gal. 6:1).

Paul wanted the individual who fell into sin restored. He did not want him censored, shamed, berated or punished; he desired the man to understand his wrongdoing and repent. Restoration was the goal. Paul knew this required the touch of a spiritually mature person to take on this task. You may be wondering, "What defines a 'spiritual' person?" In the previous chapter of Galatians, Paul contrasted those who walked by the spirit with those who walked by the flesh. In this discussion, he specifically delineated the attributes of the Christian who walked by the Spirit.

> But the fruit of the Spirit is love, joy, peace, patience, kindness, goodness, faithfulness, gentleness, self-control; against such things there is no law. Now those who belong to Christ Jesus have crucified the flesh with its passions and desires. If we live by the Spirit, let us also walk by the Spirit (Gal. 5:22-25).

A "spiritual" person is one who possesses the fruit of the Spirit. Note that "gentleness," one of the fruit of the Spirit, was a needed attribute of the spiritual person who was to restore the man who fell into sin in Galatians 6:1.

The "fruit of the Spirit" is a product of God's Spirit working inside of us. When we choose to "live by the Spirit," the Holy Spirit becomes the source of our spiritual life, which allows for the development of the "fruit of the Spirit" within us. We then, in turn, "walk by the Spirit" and let the "fruit" guide our behaviors. For example, a kind-hearted person will produce kind words when dealing with a troubled individual. In Chapter 4, it was noted that inspired Scripture equips us "for every good work" (2 Tim. 3:17). Paul knew that God's Word does not work in isolation when it comes to our spiritual formation. The Bible helps us cognitively understand what God wants us to do, but the Spirit works with God's Word (as well as with the other spiritual disciplines) to prepare willing hearts to engage in good deeds. The details of how this works are beyond the scope of this book, but it is important to understand that the rich teachings and stories in Scripture are foundational to the Spirit's work in transforming hearts, when we desire to take on the image of Christ. As the "fruit of the Spirit" progressively develops inside of us, we become spiritually prepared to engage in more and more good deeds. Let's look at each of those listed in Galatians 5:22-23 as to how they may contribute to our benevolent efforts.

Love

Love serves two basic purposes when we engage in good deeds. First, it provides the impetus to act. We see the needs of others, and "love" holds their circumstances in warm regard to the extent that we will sacrifice our own desires for their sake if it is required (Phil. 2:3-4). Jesus served as the ultimate example of this type of love by going to the cross in our stead.

Secondly, love brings to bear the other needed fruit of the Spirit as we conduct the good deed. Like a conductor of a symphony, love calls forth and harmonizes the various fruit as they work in unison to carry out the benevolent activity. For example, because we care about someone who is going through a rough time, "love" brings forth kind words, gentle ways, while exhibiting patience during that person's time of stress. Paul mentioned earlier in Galatians 5 that it is "through" love that we "serve one another" (v. 13). In 1 Corinthians 13, Paul aptly pointed out that love is the lynch pin through which all other aspects of our Christian walk must work. He said that speech without love is like "a noisy gong or a clanging symbol" (v. 1). If you can remember the most annoying sound you have ever heard your child (or a child) make, that is what your words sound like if they are not coming from a loving heart. He adds that if you have remarkable gifts, knowledge, and faith, you are "nothing" if you do not have love to accompany these wonderful things (v. 2). Even extreme self-sacrifice will "profit" you "nothing," if it is done without loving intent (v. 3). Paul then mentioned a number of qualities that love does or does not produce when it is present.

> Love is patient, love is kind *and* is not jealous; love does not brag *and* is not arrogant, does not act unbecomingly; it does not seek its own, is not provoked, does not take into account a wrong

suffered, does not rejoice in unrighteousness, but rejoices with the truth; bears all things, believes all things, hopes all things, endures all things (1 Cor. 13:4-7).

Love should be the driving force that calls forth the necessary qualities and then harmonizes them together to produce our thoughts, speech, and actions. When Christians engage in good deeds, they must be engaged in love.

Please remember, we are to love others like we love ourselves. We cannot properly love others if we do not love ourselves. I am not talking about some sort of self-righteousness. We need to value who we are in Christ Jesus. Each of us is remarkably loved by our God. When we have not forgiven ourselves of some past sinful activity, it is likely we will hold ourselves in disdain. Can we not forgive that individual in the mirror if God has forgiven us? God's loving action through His Son enables us to love ourselves again. We need to take advantage of that forgiveness, then forgive ourselves and let the loving begin.

Joy

Often people equate *joy* with happiness. Happiness is a fleeting human emotion that occurs due to a cheerful stimulus. For example, when my son or daughter comes home for the weekend, my wife and I are happy to see them, but when they leave, we experience a little sorrow. However, at their departure, our joyful nature does not leave with them. We still view life through the lens of joy even if circumstances make us temporarily unhappy. Joy as described in God's Word is a state of being. A joyful state is what allows Paul to experience life's low moments "as sorrowful" while still "always rejoicing" (2 Cor. 6:10). Life may beat us up pretty badly at times, but our joy can persevere because its source is the "God of hope" and comes about because of our belief and faith in Christ Jesus (Rom. 15:13; Phil. 1:25). Such joy creates a powerful hope within us in obtaining God's promises because of the work of God's Spirit.

A good friend of mine radiates joy whenever you encounter her. When chatting with her, you might come to understand some of her sorrows, but she always frames them in joy. Her positive view of life often causes me to entertain new perspectives, and at times even brings about contentment. One thing she does not do is steal my joy or ever leave me depressed. I want people like that in my life. She puts chocolate chips in my vanilla ice cream, if you know what I mean. So let your good deeds come from a joyful heart that is gladly willing to serve and love on others whatever the circumstances.

Peace

Many times when others need our help, their lives are full of turmoil, stress, and chaos because of the problems they are facing. In such situations, the quality of *peace* will come in handy as you reach out to them. I have encountered a few individuals in my life whose presence exude peace. Their demeanor, advice, and how they approach particular problems often bring about tranquility. Those who have found peace in Christ's love can also offer a vision of hope for peace and harmony for the downtrodden. The last thing anyone wants when dealing with difficult problems tends to be for someone to burden them with negativity and more stress, kind of like Job's friends did with their errant theology and bad advice. Peacemakers are not only blessed, they are a blessing.

Patience

For most of us, *patience* seems to be a slowly ripening "fruit." In a culture where microwaves rapidly heat our food and pain-relievers quickly numb our aches and pains, we tend to want things accomplished in an instant. Patience is a counter-cultural construct in the U.S. Nevertheless, when it comes to engaging in good deeds with others, you may need to be in it for the long-haul. I have a friend who is confrontational. His frankness comes across harshly and has resulted in damaging many of his relationships, and he's found it difficult to change. I have tried not to constantly browbeat him, but to offer him constructive alternatives on how to address certain situations. God exhibits a lot of longsuffering with our weaknesses. Can we not extend that to others as well?

Kindness

Have you ever been around someone who is utterly kind; where *kindness* is second nature to them? They make life so pleasant and enjoyable. But what happens when someone of the opposite nature enters the picture? When I worked on the Space Shuttle Program, I hated working all the shift work. Much of it involved babysitting our system in one of the Firing Rooms, when it was powered on to support testing. Since I didn't want to be on an off-shift anyway, I especially dreaded the next eight hours when I entered the Firing Room and saw a particular colleague sitting at the console. Every sentence he spoke was full of anger and bitterness. No matter how positive anyone tried to spin something, he immediately figured out how to turn it into a negative. He made life miserable.

On the contrary, I will never forget a lady from my church. She had the amazing ability to bring kind words into the bleakest of conversations. I loved talking to her. You felt uplifted being in her presence. She was the "anti-negative Firing Room guy."

When we engage in good deeds with others, we should bring kindness to bear on their circumstances: kind words, kind actions, and kind deeds. By this, you will hopefully ease some of their burdens by your caring touch.

Goodness

Goodness brings a heart of moral excellence into our good deeds, allowing those we help to see God at work in our lives and as a result in their life. Goodness goes beyond what justice demands, addressing the deeper needs of the individual. In the parable of the "Laborers in the Vineyard," Jesus explains His rationale for giving equal payment to all the laborers even though some worked more than others. He said,

> ...Friend, I am doing you no wrong; did you not agree with me for a denarius? Take what is yours and go, but I wish to give to this last man the same as to you. Is it not lawful for me to do what I wish with what is my own? Or is your eye envious because I am generous? (Matt. 20:13-15)

The word translated as "generous" above is the adjective form for the word translated as "goodness" in the list of the fruit of the Spirit in Galatians. Thus, a good heart is a generous heart. We need to stand ready to be generous, when a good deed demands it.[19]

Faithfulness

Faithfulness deals with our trustworthiness and loyalty with regard to our relationships and in following through on our commitments. When performing a good deed, we often discover that others may not want us to broadcast their problems or how we helped them. We need to understand and respect their desires concerning such things. If we ever break confidentiality with them, we probably will not be trusted in the future. Also, if we ever tell someone we will do something for them, we need to make sure we follow through. Not too long ago, I was asked to write an article for my congregation's fiftieth anniversary. I agreed and started expending a lot of mental energy on how I would put it together. Unfortunately, my week got suddenly cluttered, and the evening the article was due, I was contacted and asked if I had completed it. Instantly, I became exremely upset with myself. I pride myself on following through on my commitments. I immediately called the individual who needed to integrate all the diverse material for the publication. In such situations, it is just not satisfying to say you are sorry "ten" times. Graciously, he gave me a little more time, and I burned the midnight oil to compose the article. In all honestly, I was tired and in no state of mind to write, but I was not going to compromise my faithfulness to accomplish this good deed. Faithfulness to others and your commitments is crucial in maintaining your fellowship with others.

Gentleness

If we had a word in the English language that incorporated the qualities of strength co-joined with a gentle nature, it would aptly convey the Greek word that is translated as *gentleness* in Gal. 5:23. Just because someone has the quality of gentleness does not mean that he cannot be assertive when necessary. His gentle nature combined with self-control keeps him from becoming aggressive. We can expect this quality to come to the forefront when we are determined to help someone through a rough period by ministering to that person with a tender touch.

Self-Control

Self-control in Scripture is often concerned with sensual passions, and we should consider our ability to avoid lusting after the person whom we desire to help. You may want to giggle at such a notion, but many members of our churches do not have mastery over such passions. In such cases, the best approach is to ask someone else to carry out the good deed or to help you perform it.

As a fruit of the Spirit, I believe self-control has a broader application than sensuality. Self-control means we also live as God desires rather than as we desire. We exhibit mastery of the "self." When we perform a good work, the individual we are trying to help may push us to our wits end. Before anger takes control and we say something that we might later regret, our self-control kicks in and causes us to cool our jets and exhibit patience.

Self-control works basically that way with the rest of the fruit of the Spirit. It allows us to sustain our ability to be kind, loving, etc. in unpleasant situations or moments.

Returning to the passage with which we started this section, Paul told the Galatians that those "who are spiritual" were the ones who should gently restore the offender, and he added, use caution so that "you too will not be tempted" (Gal. 6:1). Paul knew that good judgment and self-control were needed when helping others work through a sin problem. If the helper is not careful, he too can fall into the clutches of the very temptation he is trying to help someone else overcome. One of my friends who is an alcoholic has a tough time talking with someone who is in the midst of a drinking problem. He would like to help, but such conversations have a tendency to cause him to lust for just one drink. Unfortunately, he cannot stop at one, and before he knows it, he is on a horrible "bender." Self-control and good judgment will help us in such instances.

Self-control will also aid the supposedly "spiritual" person to prevent thinking too highly of himself. Repressing any self-righteous tendencies, self-control places the emphasis on God's using us as an instrument to help others. In other words, it is all about God, not us.

Another Beloved Disciple

The Apostle John referred to himself indirectly in his Gospel as the disciple "whom Jesus loved" (John 13:23; 19:26; 20:2). When the apostles shared the Last Supper with Jesus, John portrayed this love in the word picture of him "reclining on Jesus' breast" (13:23). Allowing John to take up such an intimate posture certainly demonstrated the caring relationship Jesus had with this "beloved disciple."

Luke also shares with us in Acts another disciple beloved by those she touched by her goodness.

Now in Joppa there was a disciple named Tabitha (which translated *in Greek* is called Dorcas); this woman was abounding with deeds of kindness and charity which she continually did. And it happened at that time that she fell sick and died; and when they had washed her body, they laid it in an upper room. Since Lydda was near Joppa, the disciples, having heard that Peter was there, sent two men to him, imploring him, "Do not delay to come to us." And Peter arose and went with them. And when he had come, they brought him into the upper room; and all the widows stood beside him weeping and showing all the tunics and garments that Dorcas used to make while she was with them. But Peter sent them all out and knelt down and prayed, and turning to the body, he said, "Tabitha, arise." And she opened her eyes, and when she saw Peter, she sat up. And he gave her his hand and raised her up; and calling the saints and widows, he presented her alive. It became known all over Joppa, and many believed in the Lord (Acts 9:36-42).

Luke's story of Tabitha provides several literary features that show her esteemed status and how loved she was by her fellow Christians in Lydda. First, Tabitha (Aramaic) and Dorcas (Greek) both mean *gazelle*. Darrel Bock points out that "*gazelle* was the metaphor for 'beloved' in Song [of Solomon] 2:9 and 8:14." Even though Joppa had a large Gentile population, most of the early converts at that point were probably Jewish, so they were unlikely to miss the correlation of Tabitha's name and the metaphor in the Song of Solomon. Most certainly, "beloved" totally described how others felt about this gracious woman. Secondly, Tabitha was the only woman referred to as a female disciple in the New Testament by use of the feminine form of the Greek word for "disciple." [20]

Third, Tabitha "was abounding with deeds of kindness and charity." This was not a person who casually performed good deeds; she was rich in them. In a business sense, her "good deeds" business was booming. The phrase "deeds of kindness" could be translated "good deeds." These are the same Greek words used by Paul in Ephesians 2:10 that talk of our purpose as Christians. Tabitha actively lived out her purpose. Her "deeds of charity" probably consisted of giving alms to the poor, as well as performing other benevolent activities for those in need.

Fourth, her deeds were not sporadic; she "continually" performed them. Carrying out good deeds was second nature to her because she genuinely cared about others. Additionally, she made garments for the widows by her own hand. She did not go to the market to buy the clothing; she selflessly used her own time to lovingly create each garment. No wonder the widows cried in Peter's presence while showing him these special garments that Tabitha made for them.[21]

Also, through Tabitha's loving nature and good deeds, she had deeply endeared herself to the disciples in Joppa, so upon her death, they expeditiously sent two men to Lydda to plead with Peter to go to Joppa without haste. Obviously, their hope was in a miracle by the hands of Peter. Lastly, Peter came. Not only did he come, God's power flowed through Peter and raised Tabitha from the dead. Something must have been truly special about Tabitha for Peter to leave the fertile mission field of Lydda and Sharon. For God to raise her from the dead, He surely wanted to communicate an important message to His people throughout the ages.

An amazing thing happens when we love others and respond to their needs. Love blossoms! Love perpetuates. Churches grow as intended. Christians become like Jesus. Tabitha is quite a role model for any church, especially one in its infancy. I'll be honest; I do not know many Tabithas. I tearfully admit that I am not a Tabitha; you are probably not either, but thank God for giving us the story of this noble woman who challenges us to press on to greater service. Tabitha's story was not handed down for us to place her on a pedestal but to emulate. God works in this world through Tabithas.

■ GOOD DEEDS TO PONDER

Sometimes change provides fresh perspectives on things and opens up new opportunities for good deeds that might have gone unnoticed under previous circumstances. Also, many churches and organizations provide programs that offer ready opportunities to engage in good deeds with others and should serve as a good training ground for our future endeavors.

New Opportunities

One man discovered that moving to a new congregation can open up unsuspecting opportunities for good deeds. He hated leaving his church of twenty plus years. He had developed many close relationships during this time, and he would dearly miss his beloved friends. Yet new horizons called him to another city, so he and his family made the painful but needed move.

After they joined a friendly church of around 250 members, he experienced an unexpected, yet freeing component to his time at church. At his former congregation, the time before and after Bible classes and the worship services was always filled with dutiful obligations and conversations with long-standing friends. However, as he started to integrate into his new church family, he realized this time before and after class and worship was now mostly free.

Looking around after worship services one Sunday, he took note of a few individuals who stood awkwardly alone during these times of fellowship unsure of what to do with themselves. This man's heart went out to these socially ill-at-ease brethren. He remembered a few times in his life when he was among a large group of people yet felt utterly alone. It was a disquieting feeling for him to say the least.

Years ago his middle school classmates chose him as "Most Friendly." Possessing such a gift opened a door for a new ministry to reach out to these socially awkward folks and befriend them. His main goals included making them feel at-ease and at-home in the congregation. Engaging them in conversation was not always easy, but over time words started flowing much easier. Befriending them had good results. He noted their attendance appeared more regular, and one of them even decided to spend some time in the mission field. We can never underestimate the potential that lies within individuals in Christ Jesus.

Matthew's Hope

After working in the apartment industry for several years, a young woman knew she needed to make a change. Her life was one of exhaustion because of her employer's incessant practice of overworking her and creating a stressful work environment by asking her to break her own personal code of ethics. Another factor also weighed heavy on her heart as she felt drawn to work with those in need, and the lyrics of a song titled "Follow You" served to remind her of this unfulfilled passion. The first line and chorus speak to her calling.

> You live among the least of these, the weary and the weak
> And it would be a tragedy for me to turn away...

> And I'll, I'll follow You into the homes of the broken
> I'll follow You into the world
> I'll meet the needs for the poor and the needy God
> I'll follow You into the world

Volunteer work was not feasible because of her state of exhaustion, so she went tearfully to God in prayer over her unfulfilled passion and situation. So God answered her prayer; her company laid her off. Initially, she felt devastated over losing her job, but she felt God was at work and knew that He "had this."

After a short time, she started volunteering at a pregnancy center. She then heard a man give a talk on the need for a transitional freeze warning shelter for the homeless. Following the presentation, she volunteered for this needful work and before long became the Executive Director for Matthew's Hope Ministries. Little did she realize at the time, but her former job served as a training ground for her beloved new role. After working in this ministry for a number of years, a warm glow comes over her as she joyfully states, "I can't imagine doing anything else."

Once only drawn to help the homeless, today she lives her dream. Her ministry helps the homeless move forward in life to become self-sustaining. They are given a "hand up" not a "hand out." They try hard not to instill helplessness that occurs when you just "give, give, give" because it can easily create a "take, take, take" mentality. Matthew's Hope does help meet some basic needs such as showers, laundry, clothes, and meals, but the homeless are given an opportunity to work to earn benefits beyond the basics. Several job options are available such as growing vegetables in the Harvest of Hope Garden, detailing cars, running the pantry or taking care of the inventory system. By working in these various areas, the homeless can earn points to buy such items as bikes and tents and can even go to transitional housing. This ministry of hope owns six houses and rents six duplexes as transitional housing for those who are learning to make it on their own.

As part of trying to help the homeless move forward,

they try to create in their new workers a good work ethic. Matthew's Hope partners with the community to help find jobs for its life-learners. One of the best restaurants in the area, Chef's Table, employs some of Matthew's Hope's up-and-comers as dishwashers and preparers. Restaurants also buy some of the vegetables grown in the football-field-sized garden, especially the lettuce. Matthew's Hope recently won a grant from the Bi-Lo grocery chain to build a greenhouse alongside their existing garden.

What once started as a freeze warning shelter that existed in the director's old church building has continued to grow and expand. Partnered with fifty other churches, a shower trailer has been constructed. They are open once a week to make the basics available to the homeless. Life recovery support groups are conducted to help the homeless work through the problems they face. They also hold a Bible study for men called the "Iron Men Group" with a similar gathering for the women.

Not only has this woman helped restore the dignity of the homeless, she has helped those in need of helping others. She puts to work fifteen to twenty volunteers from her own church. Whether overseeing what and when to plant the vegetables in the garden, serving meals, coordinating medical needs, or running errands, these volunteers have all grown in various ways. From learning how to love on our culture's outcasts to selflessly helping these human beings recover from some poor life decisions, these volunteers have learned to serve. As they reach out and help others, new lasting relationships are developed. They have become the hands and feet of Jesus in this often harsh world. Focusing on evangelism is not required in this benevolent ministry because they are often asked, "Why are you doing this?"

Sharing with them about Jesus just naturally flows.

Matthew's Hope—Providing hope for the homeless and hope for developing serving spirit's in God's people.

Questions

1. Why do believers engage in good deeds, and how do they relate (or not relate) to God's plan of salvation?

2. What opportunities to engage in good deeds stir your interests?

3. Who benefits, and how, when you accomplish a good deed?

4. Of what urgent or pressing needs of others are you currently aware? Is there anything you can do to ease their burden?

5. How do our relationships impact our opportunities to perform good deeds? What might you do to grow better relationships?

6. How does the "fruit of the Spirit" come into play when we engage in good deeds? Give an example.

7. Explain the kind of impact a Tabitha (ref. Acts 9:36-42) can have on a congregation.

CHAPTER 6

Stimulating Propositions

**Do not withhold good from those to whom it is due,
when it is in your power to do it.**

(Prov. 3:27)

The selection of my guided research topic was at hand. As I stepped into my faculty advisor's office at the Harding School of Theology, my heart raced with the anticipation of receiving permission to launch this significant project on the subject of spiritual formation. Learning what God has put in place to develop His people into the likeness of His Son has always been of great interest to me. And of course, such research not only had an academic bent but held much promise for future practical applications in my desired ministry. We had hardly started discussing this research topic, when this scholastic hero of mine stated, "Mike, I know you have taught and spoken on angels in the past, why not center your research in that area?" In a nanosecond, my countenance changed from eagerness to that of concern. Even though I find angels fascinating, I saw such a project as purely an intellectual exercise with not much spiritual value. Of course intellectual and academia obviously go hand-in-hand, but I wanted my research to have a spiritual component. Prior to leaving his office, he asked me to think about and pray over it for a few days.

To be honest, I was devastated. My life would be consumed in the coming months by this project and thinking about working in an area almost devoid of any practical spiritual value caused me a great deal of anguish. Although my heart was not in it, I started anew and began to read the many passages about the angels in the Bible, seeking desperately to come up with a fresh perspective while praying for God's guidance.

As I was deliberating over my conundrum, I recalled the challenge of a gentleman years earlier. At the end of our worship service on a particular Sunday morning, one of the elders announced that I would be teaching a class on angels in the coming weeks. Afterward, a faithful member of that church approached me with a concerned look and asked, "Why are you teaching a class on angels? If it does not have anything practical in it, then it is useless." I responded that "believing in angels is a matter of faith, and with the many speculative beliefs about them in the religious world and our society, understanding what the Bible has to say about them is important." Although his comments were expressed negatively, his point was valid. I tried to introduce a few practical aspects where possible in the class, but I must admit, it was not much more than an intellectual exercise to satisfy the curious; spiritual meat was not on the menu.

While this truth haunted my thoughts once again, I asked myself, *How can such an extensive topic like the angels in the Bible not produce more spiritual fruit?* As this question intruded on my prayers and studies, God suddenly opened my mind to a new way of viewing these "angel stories." That was the problem. They were not "angel stories"; they were "God stories!" The angels were delivering His messages, executing His judgments, extending His compassion, and delivering His people. When viewing these stories through this new lens, they took on a spiritually rich perspective. Thus my guided research topic became "What Angels Tell Us About God" which led to my first book, *An Angel's View: Encountering God Through the Stories of the Heavenly Hosts.*

Why share this story? Neither my Guided Research nor my first book would have come about without the "stimulating" suggestions and comments of these two individuals. "Stimulation's" fresh perspectives may skew our view to reveal new and different horizons. Stimulation may also open doors of opportunity for service and good works. I believe God's Spirit works through men like those above to provoke our hearts into action, aligning our wills with His to bring about goodness in the lives of others.

Loving Provocation

Stimulation is a key component of church life. The gears of a congregation's good works machinery start to turn when stimulation occurs. Churches thrive when loving provocation exists, and God's people rise up to support one another. The Hebrews writer thoroughly understood this.

> and let us consider how to stimulate one another to love and good deeds, not forsaking our own assembling together, as is the habit of some, but encouraging *one another*; and all the more as you see the day drawing near (Heb. 10:24-25).

Desiring to focus the attention of his audience, the author of Hebrews launched this core teaching with the phrase, "let us consider." His direction for them was extremely important and required thoughtful consideration. He wanted them to devote some serious mental energy on "how to stimulate one another to love and good deeds." The level of intensity to this command was also highlighted by use of the power-packed word rendered *stimulate*. This was the same word used in a negative sense that described the severe disagreement between Barnabas and Paul over John Mark that caused the two to split up (Acts 15:39). In Heb. 10:24, the "stimulation" took on a positive tone though still laden with intensity; an intensity that springs forth from a heart that deeply cares for others. Such loving inducement sets its aim on breaching the superficial layers of our hearts and stirs them into loving action. Specifically, the love stirred expresses itself in good deeds.

The writer goes on to define the framework that existed for how this "stimulation" was to come about—"assembling together." By abandoning (forsaking) the body life of the church, the core purpose of expressing love for one another by performing good deeds was horribly at risk. For a season, one might grow spiritually in isolation, but our ongoing Christian walk should involve one's community of believers. We are to stand by and support one another in times of need.

Florida contains large regions that have extremely sandy soil. Sand pines thrive in these sandy environments. To withstand the storms they endure, sand pines often grow in close proximity to one another, and their roots become nested together. In such a way, they support each other when high winds assail them. A sand pine in isolation will blow over much easier than one supported by other surrounding trees. The same holds for us Christians. When life's storms rage, we need to bear the burden together, which increases our chances of coming through these turbulent times still standing.

Forms of Loving Provocation

Stimulating others to love and good deeds may take on many forms. Some of these present themselves when we assemble together. The author of Hebrews was not trying to limit good deed provocation to the four walls of our churches, as he was drawing attention to the problems that arise when our brothers and sisters stop meeting together at the appointed times. Nevertheless, most of the stimulating that occurs outside our assemblies actually has its roots in our times together. Let's take a look at some stimulating options.

Stimulating Preaching and Teaching

Many of our preachers and teachers serve as excellent stimulators because of their motivational styles. They most certainly have the venues to prick their audience's hearts. Preaching and teaching may actually take on several sub-forms of stimulating one's brothers and sisters to good deeds. Preachers and teachers may make a general appeal for the need to perform good deeds while trying to create a passion for various areas of vital work. They also might address a particular area of work that is on their heart. For example, after visiting the home of an individual from a poor area of his city, a preacher may be appalled by the undesirable living conditions he encountered and focus a sermon on the different ways his congregation might reach out to the poor. A teacher may choose to zero in on an actual need that exists in the church. For instance, after looking at some passages concerning helping widows, the teacher could organize a work party to perform some yard-work for a recently widowed sister.

A church may have an upcoming benevolent activity or program that they want to promote, so the preacher may address a congregation's need to be involved in such good works. Some churches have set aside time to paint the homes of the needy in their community. Within the sermon the preacher might mention the many ways the congregation's members can serve as well, noting the spiritual benefits that can result from their involvement. At other times, a sermon or class may emphasize the attitudes behind the good works that we set out to perform. Jesus did this very thing when He washed the apostles' feet at the Last Supper. He chose a relevant and specific good deed to perform, but the goal of that deed was much higher than clean feet.

> Jesus, knowing that the Father had given all things into His hands, and that He had come forth from God and was going back to God, got up from supper, and laid aside His garments; and taking a towel, He girded Himself. Then He poured water into the basin, and began to wash the disciples' feet, and to wipe them with the towel with which He was girded. So He came to Simon Peter. He said to Him, "Lord, do You wash my feet?" Jesus answered and said to him, "What I do you do not realize now, but you will understand hereafter." Peter said to Him, "Never shall You wash my feet!" Jesus answered him, "If I do not wash you, you have no part with Me." Simon Peter said to Him, "Lord, then wash not only my feet, but also my hands and my head." Jesus said to him, "He who has bathed needs only to wash his feet, but is completely clean; and you are clean, but not all of you." For He knew the one who was betraying Him; for this reason He said, "Not all of you are clean." So when He had washed their feet, and taken His garments, and reclined at the table again, He

said to them, "Do you know what I have done to you? You call Me Teacher and Lord; and you are right, for so I am. If I then, the Lord and the Teacher, washed your feet, you also ought to wash one another's feet. For I gave you an example that you also should do as I did to you. Truly, truly, I say to you, a slave is not greater than his master; nor is one who is sent greater than the one who sent him. If you know these things, you are blessed if you do them" (John 13:3-17).

What a remarkable scene! John's imagery takes us into the room with Jesus and the apostles. One actually can picture Jesus on His knees graciously washing their feet, as they all agonizingly look on in absolute shock and perhaps shame. You can feel Peter squirming in his seat, when Jesus kneels at his feet. John tells us that Jesus "loved them to the end" (v. 1), and so He did. By washing their feet, He displayed an extravagant yet humble love for His beloved friends. Of course, the ultimate degree of His love would soon be displayed on the cross.

Let's not be led into believing that we must physically per- form the practice of foot-washing today. It pertained to a custom of Jesus' day. Many of the roads around Jerusalem in the first century were dirty, dusty, and at times muddy, and sometimes animal feces got mixed in with the dirt and mud. People went into dinner, where everyone "reclined" at a low table (or block of wood) to eat the meal. This involved propping oneself up on an elbow while lying horizontally on your side. Your free hand was then utilized to eat the meal (without utensils) as everyone else reclined around the table with you. This left everyone's feet behind the person they were positioned by. As you might imagine, street-dirtied feet could become quite disgusting and therefore not too appetizing at mealtime. So, the practice of washing feet came about to address this pungent problem. Per the custom, a servant would typically meet the dinner guests at the door and wash their feet. For homes without a servant, one of the early guests would often take on this task. With our paved roads and wonderful transportation capabilities in the U.S., you could see why such a tradition is no longer necessary.[22]

As Jesus and the apostles were reclined around the table, hungry and ready to start what would be their last meal together, the smell of nasty feet undoubtedly filled the air. Yes, their feet needed washing, but Jesus' actions went right to the crux of the matter—their attitudes. They viewed themselves as too good for such menial work. No way was any one of them going to lower himself to wash another's feet. I remember years ago at a church I attended, we signed up for various tasks, such as vacuuming, cleaning the bathrooms, and taking care of the Lord's Supper. When I was a young adult, I remember having a haughty attitude about cleaning the restrooms. I felt I was above the distasteful task of cleaning toilets that others had used. At some point as I continued to spiritually mature, my heart changed regarding that matter, and to my family's chagrin, the only job that I ever signed us up for was cleaning the bathrooms. It was a reminder that my calling was that of a servant, and no job was beneath me. I also had a responsibility to my children to help develop in them the proper attitudes. Jesus, as the apostles' Lord and Teacher, took on an unthinkable task in their haughty minds by performing the role of a menial servant and washing their feet. Jesus' point was that if such a task was *not* too lowly for the Lord, then how could it ever be too lowly for them? By a crucial attitude adjustment, Jesus stimulated and opened their hearts to all sorts of additional good deed possibilities.

Jesus summed up His lesson with this statement: "If you know these things, you are blessed if you do them." Or in other words, "If we see a brother or sister in need, no good deed should ever be too lowly for us. Let a caring and humble attitude drive us into loving service." "Knowing" by itself produces no lasting joy and in turn leaves us unfulfilled. Only when we carry out and *experience* the good deeds we are called to perform will joy ("blessed") fill our hearts. Why wait? Be blessed!

Stimulating Examples

In past chapters, we have studied the value of role models and mentors. We also looked at the benefits of performing good deeds in the light for others to observe, realizing that God is the One to be glorified, not us. Let's quickly reiterate a potential result of such examples in our lives. Seeing a good deed in action or just becoming aware of its accomplishment has the power to "stimulate" us into action or to start thinking about future possibilities. For instance, when someone starts cleaning up after a fellowship at church, before you know it, a host of others see the need and start to help in various capacities, such as vacuuming, washing dishes, cleaning the tables, taking out the trash, and restoring the room to its normal configuration. Never underestimate the influence that a good deed may have on the behaviors of others. Some may desire to follow in our footsteps, while others' consciences may be provoked to consider future possibilities to help others. Most of us understand how the example of others can impact our future behaviors, whether good or bad. Gatorade surely understood this concept as they enticed the viewers of their commercial a number of years ago to "be like Mike." Going back and forth between Michael Jordan's acrobatic basketball moves and the children trying to emulate him, the commercial took viewers to its ultimate goal; "be like Mike," "drink Gatorade." Let's emulate Jesus in our works and perhaps others will want to do the same and come to drink a little "living water."

At NASA, we were taught that if we wanted to change the culture of our workforce, our leaders not only had to embrace the change verbally, but it needed to be visibly seen in their behaviors as well. If a church desires to stimulate its membership to love and good deeds, the leadership and ministerial staff *must* lead the way by providing good examples. One of my friends remarked to me recently that he had a pleasing image emblazoned on his memory. Many years ago, he saw one of the elders from his church on the roof of the house of one of his neighbors. He said, "I hardly know this neighbor and here one of the leaders of my church is helping him solve a problem with his roof. He not only serves the members of his church but the members of the community as well." Hold fast to those memories of those who freely serve; they can spur us on to help others as well. If our church leaders are not providing us with good examples, it begs the question: "To what examples have our members turned?"

Stimulating Announcements

Announcements at the end of our worship services, in church bulletins, or posted on a church's Facebook page provide an excellent means to stimulate one another to become involved in good deeds. Time and again, I have seen brothers and sisters step up to meet the needs of others through the means of these sources. I've seen requests for furniture, beds, food, disaster relief funds, Bible camp fees, Bibles, and other needs all be met because of an announced or published need. True Christians want to give when they can. They just need to know about the opportunities. One of the duties of leadership in our congregations is to assure the lines of communication for good deeds operate effectively and stay open. Certain circumstances may require a particular need be handled discreetly, but by the proper wording and management of the matter, even needs such as these can still be made known. Remember, the heartfelt blessings received by giving and performing good deeds are crucial to our spiritual development.

Announcements also alert us to many upcoming good works that require multiple volunteers and may involve signing up for a particular item or activity. Teaching opportunities, bringing meals to the ill or bereaved, work parties, and buying Christmas presents for children in need are but a few of the many activities churches may mobilize its members to undertake. Let's make sure that we pay attention to the various means in which our congregations notify us of the array of good works available to us. Surprisingly, many people pick up a bulletin each week but never take the time to read them. Verbal announcements at the end of a worship service may only highlight a few of the opportunities to help or serve others, so let us make sure that we take a few minutes to read through our bulletins.

From an announcement at church several years back, my wife and a close friend learned of a need for additional help in our church's food pantry and started discussing the good merits of the activity, when one of them blurted out; "Hey, let's both volunteer." The mutual encouragement that initially spawned their involvement resulted in years of joyful work, good fellowship, and a new appreciation for each other and the needs of the poor.

Spurring on Each Other

The relationships we develop at our congregations not only help us to become aware of needs, but they also allow us to learn of one another's strengths, interests, skills, and experiences. This knowledge may be useful when a particular need arises. Depending on the situation, we may be able to stimulate a brother or sister to lend a hand with someone's problem, such as in the following example. Several years ago, my wife encountered a beleaguered elderly woman exiting a grocery store carrying a couple bags of provisions. The woman boldly asked my wife if she would give her a ride home. She explained that she had walked about 5 miles to the store and was worried whether she could bear up under the heat while carrying her groceries and make it back to her home. My wife agreed, and when they arrived at the woman's trailer, my observant other-half noted that the stairs leading up to the lady's front door were falling apart. Believing they were unsafe, she brought it to my attention later that day. Unfortunately, I am not much of a carpenter, but I had a buddy who was a phenomenal handyman. He was also the most zealous good deed doer I have ever known. Only minor stimulation was needed to get him involved, and later that afternoon we arrived at the lady's trailer ready to take care of her steps. After explaining who we were and why we were there, we asked permission to dismantle her dilapidated stairway and install a new one. I'll never forget the tears of gratitude in this woman's eyes after we completed the task. Good deeds often produce such responses.

Some circumstances may require a little more communication and coordination than others. Many issues may be of a personal nature. In such cases, you always need to ask permission before trying to bring in help from a third party. For instance, I had a fellow Christian come to me and ask if I would consider helping someone who was dealing with a pornography problem. Before talking to me, he had already checked with the young man to see if he was willing to accept the help and whether it was all right to make me aware of his problem. One may need to ask the potential helper whether he or she is willing to assist before mentioning names to the person facing the problem. A number of reasons may cause them to turn down the cry for help. Obviously, that has the potential to create animosity between the two, so it is always better to check with the potential helper before revealing any names. It will be incumbent on us to use good judgment in such cases, but stimulating others to perform good works is worth the deliberation and coordination.

Jesus encountered a number of people who sought Him out to perform some type of good work, but on one occasion, He, too, experienced a little stimulation. Jesus, His mother, and His disciples attended a wedding in Cana of Galilee (John 2:1-11). These were often week-long celebrations, and wine was typically served throughout the festivities. The groom was responsible to ensure an adequate amount of wine remained available to the end of the celebration. To run out of wine at such an event in Jesus' day would have been socially humiliating for the bride and groom. Knowing this to be the case, Mary noticed that they had run out of wine and said to Jesus, "They have no wine." The text does not insinuate that she expected a miracle, so as D. A.

Carson astutely surmised, "It is more likely that Mary turned to Jesus because she had learned to rely on his resourcefulness." Whatever the case, Mary placed her faith in her Son and asked the servants to do "whatever He asks." Only for the eyes of those around Him to see, Jesus turned water into an excellent wine and averted the hosts' potential shame. It was Jesus' decision to perform this miracle but would we expect anything else of Mary than to stimulate her beloved Son to love and good deeds? [23]

Gifted Motivators

I have noticed through the years that most congregations contain a person or two who are gifted motivators. These individuals are well-networked in their church. They tend to know a lot of the members and remember little details involving their histories, skills, hobbies, and strengths. When the gifted motivator encounters someone with a pressing need beyond their ability to help or fully resolve, they go through their mental database of Christians to see if they know of someone suited to take on this particular good deed. When it comes to stimulating others to love and good deeds, they have few inhibitions about going to their brothers and sisters in Christ and offering up a little loving provocation. In fact, motivating others is often a pleasant task for them. These gifted motivators also tend to be active good deed doers themselves. We should never think they are shirking their Christian duty when they stir the hearts of others to serve those in need, because their plates are typically already full. God bless these gifted motivators; they perform a much-needed service.

Motivating a Queen

King Ahasuerus in 486 to 465 B.C. ruled the Persian Empire that extended from Ethiopia (Cush) to India (ref. The Book of Esther). On the last day of a lavish banquet in Susa, the capital city of the Empire, the king commanded that Queen Vashti come before the people and princes "to display her beauty" (v. 1:11). After the queen refused to parade herself at the banquet, the king was enraged, and probably humiliated, so he decided to remove her as queen. The king then sought a beautiful young woman to succeed Vashti as queen.

Living in exile in Susa during this time was a Jew named Mordecai. He had taken in his orphaned cousin, Esther, and was raising her "as his own daughter" (v. 2:7). Because of her beauty, Esther was chosen to undergo a year-long beautification program prior to going to the king. Once Esther went before the king, he fell in love with her and selected her as his new queen. During all this time, Esther never revealed her Jewish ancestry per instructions from Mordecai.

Following these events, the king appointed Haman as second in command, and all the king's servants were expected to bow and pay homage to Haman. However, Mordecai refused to bow before him, so in his intense hatred, the prideful Haman desired not only to kill Mordecai but all the Jews throughout the empire. Haman then devised a scheme that would bring the death of all the Jews by basically corrupting the king's judgment with a large amount of money. So the king sent out a decree that would bring death to all the Jews throughout the empire in eleven months.

When Mordecai learned of this monstrous decree, he put on sackcloth and ashes and "wailed loudly and bitterly" in the city up to the king's gate (vv. 4:1-2). Esther "writhed in great anguish" at this news as well (v. 4:4). Esther communicated with Mordecai through one of her servants, and he instructed her, like a father would a daughter, "to go in to the king to implore his favor and to plead with him for her people" (v. 4:8). This plan came with great risk to the young queen. If she went to the king when not summoned, she could be put to death, unless the king showed mercy and extended his golden scepter. Consequently, Esther communicated back to Mordecai of her apprehension.

Knowing he needed to overcome Esther's fear, Mordecai sent back the following stern message hoping to raise the stakes a little and provoke her into action.

> Then Mordecai told them to reply to Esther, "Do not imagine that you in the king's palace can escape any more than all the Jews. For if you remain silent at this time, relief and deliverance will arise for the Jews from another place and you and your father's house will perish. And who knows whether you have not attained royalty for such a time as this?" (Esther 4:13-14)

In essence, Mordecai was trying to communicate that if she was not killed due to the decree, God would still deliver His people, and as a result of her silence, God's justice would call for her life and those of her father's household. If that was not a powerful enough incentive for her to act, Mordecai then strongly suggested that perhaps God had providentially placed her in this position to foil this diabolical plan.

Mordecai succeeded in stirring the young queen into action as she went boldly forward with a plan to thwart Haman's scheme. Her brave actions saved the Jews throughout the kingdom. You can read this thrilling episode of Jewish history by reading the complete book of Esther. Without Mordecai's passionate stimulation, there is no reason to believe that Esther would have acted on her own. Stimulating others to love and good deeds can have remarkable consequences, especially as our God works in and through His people to accomplish His purposes. Perhaps this very day, you as well have been readied "for such a time as this."[24]

Esther's trepidation reminded me of my son during his preteen years. He liked stability, so trying new things always came a little hard for him. Some extra stimulation was often necessary. When the time came to remove the training wheels from his bike, he nervously protested. To him, things were fine, so why take off the wheels that kept him upright and safe? To motivate him to try it out, I promised to hold onto the bike and run alongside him until he got the feel of it without the training wheels. I finally convinced him, so off we went. When I finally let go, he was doing great. He regrettably turned his head slightly back toward me as he joyfully shouted, "You were right; this is fun!"…and then ran off the sidewalk and into the bushes. But after tasting this new freedom, he was quickly ready to try again.

■ GOOD DEEDS TO PONDER

Love may show itself in spontaneous actions or in intentional, well-planned ways. Love may confront us from unexpected sources and may take a long time to develop. When loving acts come our way, we feel valued and know that others care about us. Love's kind acts and patient perseverance can yield extraordinary results in the lives of all impacted. This is illustrated in the following two stories.

Love in an Envelope

Darkness loomed over her life. Drugs had stolen her husband and replaced her as his lover. What was created to relieve physical pain had changed this man into a different person. Driven by uncontrollable cravings, her husband stole from his once-cherished bride to support his habit and incessantly lied to her in attempts to cover his tracks. Not only had she lost her priority in his life, but their children lost a father as well. In her determination to revive their marriage, she at first separated from her husband and then convinced him to go to counseling with her. Still unable to admit to his problem, his bad behaviors continued. She wanted to help him, but he did not want help. She then pursued divorce, because it appeared to be the only course of action.

He was stealing her credit and debit cards, which caused financial problems. As a bank teller at a regional bank, she was held to a higher standard when it came to her credit standing and overdrawing of her accounts was not tolerated. Between the expectations of her job, the financial demands of raising her children as a single mom, a mountain of debt, and the bills that kept coming in, she was under tremendous financial stress. Nevertheless, she said to herself, "I can do this." Using her training in budgeting and her gift of self-discipline, she committed to ethically raise her children and work through all the difficulties. She and her children lived day-to-day adhering to a strict budget. Every aspect of their life became impacted; the utilities they used, the clothes they wore, the food they ate, and everything that required cash was subject to a rigid budget. The children neither complained nor asked for anything, because this loving mother helped them understand their financially stressed situation. Responsibilities of a single mom run deep and bring about an anguish few of us can understand.

One Sunday, the single mom's mother came by her home and handed her a sealed blank envelope. Earlier that morning, someone at church handed it to her and asked her to pass it on to her daughter. Not knowing what was in it or who it actually came from, her daughter stared at the envelope with a perplexed look. As she opened the envelope, she saw its only contents—$100. The single mom said, "Wow!" then proceeded to cry. She immediately spent it on some pressing bills, and the envelope's blessing started to reduce some of her stress.

A month later, another hundred dollars came in a blank envelope. This time she spent half of it on bills and then bought her daughters some much needed clothing. One of her children asked, "Is this okay?" Mom answered, "Yes, we have received a blessing from someone." The children were happy and so was mom. The envelopes came for approximately eight months, and she never knew their gracious source. After the third envelope, she decided to write a thank-you letter to the anonymous giver. Tears uncontrollably flowed down her cheeks, as she expressed her extreme gratitude and explained how helpful the money had been. In humble words, she told the donor that "they were an angel, a blessing sent by God." Thanking the donor over and over in her letter, she marveled at the thought behind the anonymous gifts. Sometimes she even reached out to others by taking some of the money and putting it in her church's collection plate on Sunday morning.

A victim of sustained lying, stealing, and manipulation, she had stopped trusting others, and negativity began to replace her previously positive approach to life. But the envelopes reminded her that good people still existed. They helped her re-engage her faith, because she knew that God was ultimately behind these kind gifts. She wanted to emulate the kind heart of the giver. Her damaged attitudes started to spiritually heal and change, prompting her to start helping others once more. What a marvelous outcome from envelopes filled with money...no, filled with love!

The Bus Driver

His church needed an additional driver to pick up children from around his city to attend its classes and worship services. He thought, *Well, I know how to drive, so I guess I can fill this need.* Driving up to three times a week, he drove the "Jesus van," as they affectionately called it, to a number of homes around the city. During the early days of his chaperoning duties, there were four brothers who religiously caught a ride, but he felt a little wary of them. A true ethnic and economic divide existed between these boys and the bus driver. In fact, he came to realize that the boys were actually trained to dislike "white people." Early on, the four brothers' behavior was deplorable. They were rude and often trouble-makers. One of them even took a swing at a female who helped with the youth group. When they wanted something, they did not ask for it politely, they demanded it. As you might imagine, their "potluck" etiquette was atrocious. They would cut in line and take more food than they could possibly eat.

The bus driver tried to help address the four brothers' bad behavior at various church and youth events, but they created so much chaos he was ready to give up on them. His wife tried to help him by stimulating him to see the world through the eyes of the four brothers. He realized that they had little hope of making it in this world without a kind, yet assertive, hand to guide them. His heart started to melt. He knew they sorely needed God's grace to take hold of their hearts, so the bus driver decided to hang in there with them. He learned to make better use of their van rides together by forcing conversations with them, and later the dialogue came much easier. He started training them in potluck etiquette and got them involved in Lads to Leaders. At one particular Lads to Leaders session, the boys really started behaving badly. Someone recognized that they were all really hungry, and thought that might be contributing to their poor conduct. So they decided to share a meal at each of these events in the future. The meals became the key to building trust and opening the hearts of the four brothers.

The bus driver helped pull together the funds that allowed the boys to go to the summer Bible and work camps. A deep bond started to develop between them, and even their parents recognized it. On one occasion, one of the boys was seriously ill and was admitted to the hospital. The parents asked the church if they could help with their other three sons, so the boys were split up and stayed in various church members' homes during the fourth brother's stay in the hospital. The church also stepped up for this family by providing the boys with new bunk beds, along with mattresses, pillows, bed linens, and bedspreads. Through the work of the youth minister, the bus driver, members of the youth group, and many others at the church, each of the boys has decided to follow Christ. The bus driver was even given the privilege of baptizing two of the boys himself.

Knowing he was no longer the same man and the four boys were not the same kids, the bus driver started to become emotionally attached to them. Those once rambunctious boys, who looked at him through jaundiced eyes when they first met him, had touched him in a profound way. He became an important part of their lives. They often include him in their decision-making processes. To him, they are like his own children. He loves them and often tells them so. They may not totally understand it now, but he knows it will help facilitate their success as Christians and as citizens. One of them now plays on the soccer team he coaches. It is the first organized sport the boy has ever played. Learning to use his remarkable speed in a sport may now open some doors for the young man to go to college in the future. Occasionally, the bus driver has the opportunity to take some of them to a restaurant. This is still an overwhelming experience for them because of all the options on the menu. For many of us, splitting a hamburger into quarters is outside of our experience base, but that was their only exposure to eating out.

To some degree, the bus driver has learned to see through

these boys' eyes. It has become quite clear how their peers, home life, ethnicity, and financial hardships have shaped their lives. Empathy for the needs of others has become a new virtue for this man, along with developing more patience...a lot more patience. The bus driver desires to be an elder in his church some day, and he knows working with these young men has helped prepare him for such a great responsibility. Perhaps most of all, he has learned that *love never fails.*

Questions

1. How is stimulating others to love and good deeds a key component of church life?

2. Can you recall a situation when someone stimulated you to do a good deed? Discuss the situation and results.

3. Have you ever stirred up someone to perform a good deed? Why did you not perform the good deed yourself?

4. From the vantage point of stimulating others to perform good deeds, why is it important to attend our churches regularly?

5. How might our preachers and teachers stimulate us to perform good deeds? What was Jesus trying to teach the apostles when he washed their feet? Does that have relevance to you today? If so, in what way?

6. Can you recall a time when you saw someone performing a good deed that stirred your heart into loving action? Explain.

7. Do you have any "gifted motivators" in your church? Explain their importance?

8. Explain the circumstances that might require the stimulation to be "stern" when we are trying to stir up someone to do a good work.

Overcoming

**Live such good lives among the pagans that, though they
accuse you of doing wrong, they may see your good deeds and
glorify God on the day he visits us.**

(1 Pet. 2:12, NIV)

E ven though I have lived in Florida nearly all of my life, I
am an unwavering Baltimore Orioles baseball fan. My dad
raised me that way, and it definitely stuck. When you think of
the attributes of a die-hard fan, they fit me to a T when it comes
to the O's. I record and watch most of the Orioles games. One
of the things you pick up on when you watch so many games is
the unwritten rules of conduct the players expect one another
to follow. For instance, when a player hits a home run, he is to
refrain from standing at home plate and admiring the ball as it
sails over the fence. Such behavior is considered bad form and a
way of showing up the pitcher. It's kind of like a non-verbal "in
your face!" If a player does this, the next time the "home run
admirer" comes up to bat, he is likely to get drilled by the pitcher
with a ninety mile per hour fastball. After that, both teams start
shouting unpleasantries at one another from the top steps of their
dugouts, as the hit batter stares down the pitcher while making his
way to first base. The umpires immediately warn both managers
that no more of this type of behavior will be tolerated. Nevertheless, the hit batter's team now seeks the right opportunity for
a little revenge. They wait until the opposing team sends one of
their better hitters up to the plate. He then is also plunked by a
fastball. Getting hit by a ninety mile per hour "heater" does not
feel pleasant at all, so as the pain begins to blur his judgment, he
may decide to charge the mound in retaliation. If so, the benches
then empty onto the field. Some players may come out swinging
while others just verbally spew their vitriol at their opponents.

Even after the game is over, the bad blood between the two teams may follow them for years to come.

I could easily change the example but similar conduct tends to permeate virtually all aspects of life around the globe. Whether spouses, politicians, co-workers, neighbors, nations, or church members, none of these seems to be immune to retaliatory behavior. When one party hurts the other, sparks often begin to fly. Sometimes events escalate so rapidly that things get out of control and result in horrific outcomes. Ultimately, vengeful behavior can result in war, murder, divorce, fights (verbal and physical), lawsuits, disloyalty, hate-filled speech, and so on. At this moment, you may be recalling such an escalating series of events that consumed your life in the past or perhaps recently. Let's look at how God's Word tells us to handle such situations and some inspirational examples.

The Key to Overcoming Evil

In Romans 12, Paul laid out for the Christians in Rome what living the transformed life looked like with regard to their service, attitudes, and morality. The last thing he addressed in the chapter was personal vengeance.

> Never pay back evil for evil to anyone. Respect what is right in the sight of all men. If possible, so far as it depends on you, be at peace with all men. Never take your own revenge, beloved, but leave room for the wrath of God, for it is written, "Vengeance is Mine, I will repay," says the Lord. "But if your enemy is hungry, feed him, and if he is thirsty, give him a drink; for in so doing you will heap burning coals upon his head." Do not be overcome by evil, but overcome evil with good (Rom. 12:17-21).

Paul hit this serious subject hard. Right out of the chute he told them *never*. After only one more verse, he succinctly rephrased the same command starting again with *never*. Paul wanted them to understand that plotting and carrying out vengeance is totally counter to the Christian lifestyle, so they needed to turn away from such vindictive pursuits.

Paul revealed his ultimate concern in verse 21 for Christians who become obsessed with seeking vengeance; following such pathways can cause evil to overcome them. Paul stated this warning to the Ephesians:

> Be angry, and yet do not sin; do not let the sun go down on your anger, and do not give the devil an opportunity (Eph. 4:26-27).

Have you ever given the devil an opportunity in this manner? Paul knew what happens when we don't readily resolve our anger. It festers and starts to breed hate. Anger then starts to consume us. It makes its home in our hearts and dwells there. We desperately want to get back at the one who hurt, misled, betrayed, embarrassed, or did whatever injurious thing to us. We want vengeance! It will overcome us if we let it. Paul said, "Never!" We must not go there!

Jesus voiced the same concern as Paul. He did not want His people to erroneously believe they were righteous just because they obeyed the law and did not commit murder, while their hearts were filled with raging anger (Matt. 5:21-24). Such hearts were not righteous, so Jesus told them to go and "be reconciled to your brother." Or in other words, "Quit letting your anger consume you; go get it out of your heart."

Paul also gives another reason why we should "never" seek revenge: It is God's place to administer justice in such matters. Our culture's short-term view of life often perverts the way we look at things. God takes an eternal perspective. Our knowledge of events and others' motives is incomplete and viewed through our own biases. God is all-knowing and unbiased. Past events have no power to shape who He is. Knowing our propensity to become consumed with vengeful scheming, God knows that vengeance is best left to Him; "'Vengeance is Mine, I will repay,' says the Lord" (Rom. 12:19). His approach to justice may not always sit well with us. We usually want immediate action, but our longsuffering God may have other goals in mind. Where others spend eternity may depend on His patience. Scripture is clear about the administration of justice for wrongs done against us; we need to leave it up to God. Civil authorities serve Him as a ministry to achieve justice, whether they realize it or not (Rom. 13:3-4). And if justice is not served in this lifetime, God will see to it when Christ returns. Eternity is a long time. [25]

At the end of this teaching, Paul gives us the key to preventing evil from overcoming us when we have been wronged by others. We can never let it acquire a foothold, "overcome evil with good" (Rom 12:21). You may be thinking, "Well that sounds fine but is that not a little abstract?" By itself, yes, but Paul just clarified what he specifically meant in verse 20. You counteract their bad behaviors with *good deeds*. Give them a drink, give them food; positively reach out to them based on their needs. You thought just ignoring them might be satisfactory, but Paul wants us to show some concern toward them by addressing their obvious needs. Is that difficult? You bet it is! Jesus' daunting command regarding this also soundly resonated with Paul's; "...love your enemies and pray for those who persecute you" (Matt. 5:44). Prior to saying this, Jesus provided a couple of examples of how to accomplish His new direction.

> But I say to you, do not resist an evil person; but whoever slaps you on your right cheek, turn the other to him also. If anyone wants to sue you, and take your shirt, let him have your coat also. Whoever forces you to go one mile, go with him two (Matt. 5:39-41).

So if a Roman soldier pressed you into service to carry his bags for a mile (as was lawful in the Roman Empire), your reaction was not to be outraged and vengeful but willing to help. [26] These commands may be the most challenging in all of Scripture. Neither you nor I can probably produce many true examples of this kind of behavior. Nevertheless, Paul has given us the recipe for overcoming evil with good. Jesus said such behavior was "so that you may be sons of your Father who is in heaven..." (Matt. 5:45). Shocking to the world though it may be, overcoming evil with good is unmistakably Christian.

In Rom 12:17, Paul described the *quality* of our reaction to an evil carried out against us. The phrase translated by the New American Standard as "Respect what is right in the sight of all men," basically means to give some forethought to your response, and when we do respond let the response be unmistakably good. Our inner goodness produces an outward goodness, so no one should ever confuse our reaction with evil.[27]

Our response to those who hurt us should produce peace, not perpetuate evil. Paul recognized that such outcomes may not always be possible. Because of the mean-spirited attitudes of some oppressors, they may want to continue in their despicable ways regardless of our responding with goodness. Even so, for us Christians, the proper responses are to forgive and pursue peace.

When Jesus was washing the apostles' feet at the Last Supper, I wonder what was on Judas's mind. Jesus knew of Judas's traitorous scheming, but He still humbly washed His betrayer's feet. He did not skip, chide, or call him names. Jesus just lovingly washed Judas's feet. Many of us might be thinking, *I would have liked to have scrubbed those traitorous feet with a piece of steel wool*, but not our Lord. He pursued a path of peace that might have softened many hearts, but Judas's greed-hardened heart was too callous to be softened. His upcoming betrayal of Christ initiated a series of events that spiraled unmercifully downward and ended with his Lord and Teacher on a Roman cross. Nevertheless, Jesus overcame the cross, and mercy now abounds and an everlasting peace is available to each of us.

In a passage where peace and overcoming evil with good were the paramount goals, one of Paul's phrases has an odd ring to our twenty-first century ears. After stating the necessity to address the needs of thirst and hunger of an oppressor, Paul followed with, "...for in so doing you will heap burning coals upon his head" (Rom 12:20). Taken literally, we might say to ourselves, "Well, I really can't stand that person who hurt me, so I am going to throw in a few extra good deeds to increase their punishment." Such spiteful thinking was obviously counter to Paul's overall teaching. Our good deeds will hopefully not only overcome the evil of our enemies and bring about peace, but also create in us a heart that contemplates good, not evil. Desiring to do good deeds to increase someone's punishment comes from a vengeful heart, which we want to preclude in the first place. So how should we interpret this phrase? Treating this expression as a metaphor appears to be the best approach. Our good deeds should bring a burning sense of shame to our offender that hopefully leads them to repentance and seeking the Lord. Paul was teaching that leading the transformed life has the hope of producing positive not negative outcomes. Let's take a look at some examples.[28]

Falling a Little Short

I remember a number of years ago at the Kennedy Space Center when I was making my way back to my office, an individual suddenly confronted me in the hallway. Her face immediately contorted like she had just bitten into a lemon, and she started into an ugly tirade. In a rabid way, accusative speech spewed out of her mouth, claiming that I had conspired against her to obtain the position that I held. She had desperately wanted that job and felt she deserved to be in it. Of course, the individual had totally misconstrued the situation. Not only had I not conspired with anyone to obtain this job, it took me over a month to decide whether I even wanted it, once the job had been offered. My personal career goals at that point had me on a different trajectory, and I reluctantly had accepted the job only to help out in a particular situation. Nevertheless, trying to reason with this person was futile, so I finally gave up and left her still foaming at the mouth in the hallway.

After that incident, this individual's hatred toward me regrettably continued, as she relayed her conspiracy theory to anyone who would listen. Subsequent to this, another manager came to me and asked me to go to one of our senior managers over another incident involving this unreasonable individual. This manager had no use for this person and wanted her out of the way. He actually stated it this way to me, "I want her killed" (metaphorically speaking). I refused to go down that path, as it violated my Christian ethics. If I was asked about the situation, I would truthfully divulge what had occurred, but I would not go to management to cause this person any trouble. My overall approach to the situation with the unreasonable individual was to ignore her, if possible, and do nothing to perpetuate the problem.

While thinking about this unfortunate situation, I became mindful of a story about David that contained some similarities to my own. King Saul believed that David was a threat to his kingdom, so Saul along with some of his elite warriors chased David and his men around the Judean countryside in an attempt to kill Israel's future king. On one occasion though, Saul unknowingly left himself completely vulnerable to the careworn David.

And he came to the sheepfolds on the way, where there *was* a cave; and Saul went in to relieve himself. Now David and his men were sitting in the inner recesses of the cave. And the men of David said to him, "Behold, *this is* the day of which the Lord said to you, 'Behold; I am about to give your enemy into your hand, and you shall do to him as it seems good to you.'" Then David arose and cut off the edge of Saul's robe secretly. And it came about afterward that David's conscience bothered him because he had cut off the edge of Saul's *robe.* So he said to his men, "Far be it from me because of the Lord that I should do this thing to my lord, the Lord's anointed, to stretch out my hand against him, since he is the Lord's anointed." David persuaded his men with *these* words and did not allow them to rise up against Saul. And Saul arose, left the cave, and went on *his* way (1 Sam. 24:3-7).

Truly caught with his pants down, Saul's life teetered on David's conscience. With his men tempting him to kill their unrelenting aggressor, David drew his sword and stealthily made his way toward the king. Whether he had a change of heart or carried out his original intention, we will never know this side of heaven. But David spared the king's life and only cut off the edge of Saul's robe.

I believe David's *inaction*, in avoiding Saul's murder, actually should be viewed as a good deed. Saul's pursuit of the innocent David was unjustifiable and purely premeditated evil. David's innate goodness kept him from striking down the "Lord's anointed." However, unlike my own situation above, where I kept my distance from the unreasonable individual, David made his kindness known to Saul as he shouted to him outside the cave. My oppressor never knew that I chose not to follow through on the other manager's mean-spirited request. To be honest though, I never really pursued peace with this person after our initial confrontation. I did her no evil, but I never tried to improve the situation by performing any good deeds. But in the case of David, he humbled himself before the king as he prostrated himself before him and referred to Saul as "My lord the king!" (v. 8). David said he took pity (or had compassion) on him (v. 10). He also referred to Saul as "my father" (v.11). This might just be in recognition of Saul's authority as the ruler, but perhaps David was fondly recalling his relationship with Saul as part of the royal family. Saul was David's father-in-law after he married the king's daughter, Michal. I believe the latter to be the case, since Saul, in turn, referred to him as "my son David" (v. 16). David used what occurred in the cave as proof of his good will towards the king. With the realization that David had returned his evil with good, Saul became emotionally broken and wept. He admitted to his wickedness and acknowledged that David would one day rule Israel. Because of David's acts of goodness, the two peaceably went their separate ways. Of course, with the spirit of confusion that came randomly upon Saul, David's grief with the king was not yet over.

In my situation, I would have betrayed a confidence had I let my oppressor know that I refused to go to senior management to cause her trouble, but honestly, it was not because I cared for this person. In fact, to the contrary, I did not care for this individual. She was hateful and known for her dreadful and self-serving behavior. My actions were driven by my personal ethic of not wanting to do something evil, rather than as an act of good will toward that person. I bring all this up, because these types of situations are stressful and tough to manage. I fell short of what God would have liked for me to have accomplished. She did not see Jesus in me; in fact, she pretty much saw nothing. As a Christian, I wish my maturity had been a little further along, and perhaps I could have acted in a more benevolent way, showing my concern for her well-being in word and deed. And maybe, she could have recognized my good will and sought why I responded to her in this way. My reply could have been, "Jesus desires me to treat others in loving ways; would you like to know more?"

Examples of Overcoming

I racked my brain for days and talked with several devout, caring Christians in an attempt to convey stories in which good deeds were carried out to overcome evil with good. I uncovered some remarkable stories of forgiveness, which is important, but I only found a couple of stories in which an individual responded to evil with good deeds. I mention this to demonstrate that to live out the edict of overcoming evil with good is extraordinarily difficult. In fact, it may be at the pinnacle of one's Christian maturity. We all need to give constant attention to what we let impact our hearts.

Davie and Abigail

While David and his men hid in the wilderness of Maon from King Saul, an interesting series of events occurred regarding the flocks of a man named Nabal (ref. 1 Sam. 25). Under David's leadership, his band of ragtag men "guarded" (v. 21) this rich man's flocks from marauders and thieves. They were not asked to perform this service, but after saving Keilah from the pillaging Philistines (see 1 Sam. 23:1-5), it was obviously a fitting thing for David to do for a fellow countryman. In fact, one of Nabal's servants acknowledged that David's men were "very good" to the shepherds, they were never "insulted," nor did they "miss anything" (v. 15). The servant added that David's men "were a wall to us both by night and by day, all the time we were with them tending the sheep" (v. 16). David viewed this as a "good" gesture on his part (v. 21).

While Nabal was having his sheep sheared in Carmel, David sent ten young men to seek provisions from him based on their noble service of protecting his flocks. The young men were to greet Nabal in David's name, extend a blessing on Nabal and his household, and mention their good relationship with his shepherds. The following was David's specific request and Nabal's response.

> ...Therefore let my young men find favor in your eyes, for we have come on a festive day. Please give whatever you find at hand to your servants and to your son David (1 Sam 25:8).

> But Nabal answered David's servants, and said, "Who is David? And who is the son of Jesse? There are many servants today who are each breaking away from his master. Shall I then take my bread and my water and my meat that I have slaughtered for my shearers, and give it to men whose origin I do not know?" (1 Sam. 25:10-11)

David's tone was one of humility, as he referred to his young men as "your servants" and himself as "your son David." Apparently, Bethlehem was founded by the Calebite clan (read 1 Chr.

2:42-51). Since Bethlehem was David's hometown and Nabal was identified as a Calebite, the two were kinsman. Robert D. Bergen believes that "David's reference to himself as Nabal's son emphasizes the kindred and amicable relationship that David believed to exist between the two Judahites."[29]

The writer already informed his readers that Nabal was "harsh and evil in his dealings," so his offensive reaction to David's request should be no surprise. First, he viewed David with contempt. You can hear the disdainful thoughts behind Nabal's response, "I am a rich businessman, who does this homeless squatter think he is?" Secondly, Nabal compared David and his men to a bunch of rogue slaves that broke away from their masters. Nabal also made eight first person references concerning himself in his terse diatribe in verse 11, highlighting his self-centered character.[30]

David felt that Nabal had returned his good deeds of protecting his flocks and shepherds with evil (v. 21). As a result, David became immediately consumed by vengeance and told his men to strap on their swords. David and four hundred men made a beeline for Nabal's estate. Now, he did not want provisions alone, he planned on slaughtering every male associated with Nabal.

Abigail, Nabal's wife, then entered the frantic scene. Described as "intelligent and beautiful" (v. 3), she desperately needed both of these qualities to deter David's raging desire for revenge. After a servant informed Abigail of how Nabal had disrespected David's men, he then gave her the following warning.

> Now therefore, know and consider what you should do, for evil
> is plotted against our master and against all his household; and
> he is such a worthless man that no one can speak to him (v. 17).

David was not willing to return Saul's evil with evil, but in Nabal's case, we see the future king's character crumble as a willingness to carry out evil consumed him. Fortunately, Abigail had a plan to alleviate David's bloodlust. She prepared a generous portion of food to deliver to David in appreciation of his protective services. However, this bountiful gift was only part of this savvy woman's plan. Let's pick up the story as she approached David on the way to Nabal's land.

> When Abigail saw David, she hurried and dismounted from her donkey, and fell on her face before David and bowed herself to the ground. And she fell at his feet and said, "On me alone, my lord, be the blame. And please let your maidservant speak to you, and listen to the words of your maidservant. Please do not let my lord pay attention to this worthless man, Nabal, for as his name is, so is he. Nabal is his name and folly is with him; but I your maidservant did not see the young men of my lord whom you sent. "Now therefore, my lord, as the Lord lives, and as your soul lives, since the Lord has restrained you from shedding blood, and from avenging yourself by your own hand, now then let your enemies and those who seek evil against my lord, be as Nabal. Now let this gift which your maidservant has brought to my lord be given to the young men who accompany my lord. Please forgive the transgression of your maidservant; for the Lord will certainly make for my lord an enduring house, because my lord is fighting the battles of the Lord, and evil will not be found in you all your days. Should anyone rise up to pursue you and to seek your life, then the life of my lord shall be bound in the bundle of the living with the Lord your God; but the lives of your enemies He will sling out as from the hollow of a sling. And when the Lord does for my lord according to all the good that He has spoken concerning you, and appoints you ruler over Israel, this will not cause grief or a troubled heart to my lord, both by having shed blood without cause and by my lord having avenged himself. When the Lord shall deal well with my lord, then remember your maidservant" (1 Sam. 25:23-31).

Wow! What an eloquent speech. Look at the respect Abigail showed David in contrast to her husband's disrespect. She bowed before him. She addressed him as her "lord" while she described herself as his "maidservant." And she recognized David as heir to the throne of Israel. These accolades served to set up her convincing plea as well as to calm the agitated young David. Time and again in Abigail's speech, you can see her intelligence and wisdom rising to the occasion. She took the blame for the incident, even though Nabal was at fault, and asked for David's forgiveness. Have you ever asked for forgiveness even when you knew you were not to blame for something? In my experience, I have found it to be extremely effective in calming down a situation, which allows good communication to flow again. In her own shrewd way, Abigail insinuated to David, "Why let such a foolish man like Nabal work you into a frenzy, as he is a 'worthless man.'" She also stated that the Lord was on David's side, and he was fighting the Lord's battles. As David slew Goliath with a sling, Abigail tactfully attempted to slay David's heart with a reference to God using a sling to assail his enemies. Abigail also subtly reproved David's ill-advised pursuit of vengeance. It was the Lord who was now restraining him, and she reminded him that he did not want such innocent bloodshed on his conscience when he became king. She ended her entreaty as she began, again referring to David as "lord" and herself as "maidservant."

Abigail averted evil with good. With his sanity now restored, David said, "Blessed be the Lord God of Israel, who sent you this day to meet me" (v. 32). David admitted that her discernment prevented him from wrongly avenging himself. Abigail pursued peace and that was what David returned to her; "Go up to your house in peace. See, I have listened to you and granted your request" (v. 35). May we all learn from the wisdom and goodness of the Abigail's of this world! They are remarkable people and worthy of our attention.

Persecution and the Pursuit of Peace

I have come to know quite a few ministers through the years, but there have only been a couple of them whom I have turned to as trusted confidants to help me constructively work through a problem. The following story involves one of those men whose gentleness, wisdom and caring spirit intertwine in a most godly way.

Years ago, a pulpit minister at a fairly established church saw the need to reach out and attract a wider group of people from their community. He proposed that their congregation conduct two worship services on Sunday mornings. One service could continue in their traditional style, while the other could strive to create a more casual atmosphere. The essence of the teachings would remain the same; the differences between the two services would only be in style. His belief was that this would allow them to expose another segment of their community to the gospel.

Some families were uncomfortable about the proposal, but one particular individual lost all confidence in this minister she had known for thirteen years. In fact, she wrote a letter to the eldership to voice her opposition to the change and referred to the minster as a "son of the devil." The elders shared the letter with the minister. He respected the disgruntled individual's opinions about the addition of the new service but was devastated by this vile slur. By no means was he perfect, but his conduct and life's service was devoted to God and to be referred to as Satan's spawn hurt and hurt deeply.

He decided to persevere through this persecution and still minister to this family. When they were sick, he took them food. When they were in the hospital, he visited them. He ministered to one of their grandchildren, supporting that family member during a serious health problem and helping them work through some tough life issues. He still cared about this family and would demonstrate it through performing good deeds as the needs arose. The minister's wife on one occasion asked him, "Why are you treating them so well after what they said about you?" He responded, "Because that is what Jesus would do in the same situation." He realized that in his position he would experience criticism at times. He in turn needed to respond in good rather than evil ways. Even after all these years, thinking about this situation brought tears to his eyes as I interviewed him...he wishes that the hurtful comment had never been made.

When the spouse of the critical person fell mortally ill, this individual asked the minister to come by their spouse's side as they passed away. He was then requested to perform the funeral. Other ministerial requests continued to come his way from this once spiteful person. He had truly overcome evil with good. Loving others may be the most powerful healing agent God ever created.

■ GOOD DEEDS TO PONDER

Advice by nature may tend to be abstract, but from a reliable and trusted source, sound advice may be one of the most concrete good deeds anyone could ever do for us. The following two stories show the significance of how advice from the right source can offer us life-changing and saving guidance.

The Counselor

Expecting the excitement of their new marriage to last forever, a youthful husband soon found that this new life with his bride was less than his ideal. His model of what married life should look like was not the reality in which he found himself living. Unfortunately, since he hated conflict, he kept his disillusionment to himself. For him, married life soon became a façade filled with lies and deceit. Avoiding potential conflict, he kept his unhappiness to himself and slowly pulled away from his once-cherished bride. He erroneously concluded that sharing the truth of his feelings would destroy things: so rather than share his thoughts and feelings, he hid them.

For the young shy bride, her husband was her everything and the only man for her. Only with him could she reveal her deepest thoughts and emotions. She felt joy and safety in his presence. As he started turning inward and "hiding," a lonely feeling started to loom over her. She lost that intimate connection with him that she cherished and needed. As he continued to pull away, the solitude grew and romantically their love started to crumble. Desperately trying to regain something she lost in her marriage, she committed a brief infidelity. Then in an attempt at reconciliation, she told her husband of her fleeting encounter with another man. This hurt him to the core, and as an unrelenting rage took hold of him, the husband's fury became his passion. He knew he should forgive her, but he did not want to let go of the anger. Blame felt better at the time, and he told her that he did not love her any longer. Eventually, all the negative feelings caused him to turn to another woman. Sadly, his infidelity occurred while his bride was pregnant with their second child.

After moving in with her parents, they began meeting with a Christian counselor together, but counseling resulted in too much conflict for him. He instead chose to pursue his career goals, and the popularity that came with that pursuit held an exalted place in his heart. He had made his career a false idol, which created an ever-present tension with his strained desire to be a good husband and parent. Things appeared to be on the mend, but then another girl entered the husband's life. Before the situation got worse, the wife demanded that he quit his job and not see the girl. She specifically asked the question, "Do you want a divorce?" Instead of answering the question, he left and no longer went to counseling. The care-worn young woman broke down. She stated, "I lost my mind for a while." Separated, now wanting a divorce, this stress-laden woman contemplated, "How do you raise children without the happiness of your partner?" Life became dark and bleak, she wondered, *Perhaps suicide is the answer.*

She started seeing her counselor twice a week. In her depressed state, she felt that she was "bad" and needed to let someone know. The counselor hung in with her through these tough times, not only seeing her twice a week but taking as many as four phone calls from her a day. The counselor's care for her went deep, and in her state of agitation, she needed his sage advice and calming influence. She could tell him anything. He never responded in shock but brought peace and tranquility into her tumultuous life. The counselor gave her hope. He pointed out that statistically her husband was likely to come back. In the counselor's care, she found a place to heal and work on her own character development. They also worked on her ability to forgive her husband, as she needed to come to a place inside her heart to allow this to happen if he came back to her. Equipped with tools to address her insecurities and shortcomings, a newly found confidence began to take hold in her, and she started to feel good about herself again. Her future had hope on its horizon, and she was learning to choose the ways of love and peace in her life.

For eighteen months, the wayward husband pursued his ambitions and kept his distance from his wife. During that time, he came to the conclusion that his dreams had misled him and realized that he was "not finding what I thought I would." He missed his wife. He longed for his children. Depression hit him hard, but he was able to start casually conversing with his wife. A strange kind of friendship evolved, and they moved into his parents' home, though staying in separate rooms. They tried co-parenting.

In the meantime, the wife continued to grow mentally and spiritually. Her newfound maturity was blossoming, and a sense of value that had eluded her for a long time began to take root. Nevertheless, she still tended to resent his first lover and harbored some disappointment with God that things had not worked out better. The wife handed him a list of things she thought needed to exist for them to be married. She said to him, "I would love you more than anyone, but I need to leave." She knew that she needed to separate herself from his unhealthy ways to sustain her love for him. She viewed him as lost and prayed for him. During this time, the husband recognized that she did not want to hate or vilify him. In fact, he realized that she still loved him, but she could not be a part of his life while he exhibited his destructive behaviors.

He eventually sought reconciliation and asked to get back together. He said, "I love you and want my family back." His wife was now terrified and mentally kept asking herself whether she could trust him. Understanding the importance of marriage, and the fact that God thinks it is important, she rallied the courage and went down a path to make amends. However, in her forgiveness, she expected him to live to a higher standard. She asked God to protect her children through the coming days as the future's outcome was a little hazy. In good faith, the husband started going to counseling again. But still a raging conflict flamed within him: Should he choose to be a good husband or pursue fame? He, too, started "losing his mind" and was driven into utter brokenness, contemplating suicide as a means of escaping his dismal dilemma. Nevertheless, the counselor's kind and tender touch started to raise him from the ashes. He finally opened up and shared his darkest parts. The counselor never became condescending or told him "I told you so" but accepted him where he was. He became a father figure to the young man. The counselor told him that he loved him, would be there for him, and reassured him that he did not have to walk this journey alone. They sifted through his problems and conflicted feelings one at a time. Ultimately, the young man came to the realization that his priority genuinely was his marriage and being a father. No longer would his career share the spotlight with or be a higher priority than his family.

The wife recognized the extreme impact of the counselor on her husband. He started to open up to her more. At first, honesty was hard for him, but he came to the realization that lying actually separates. For their marriage to thrive, it would be incumbent on him to exhibit the same kind of transparency with his wife that was needed between himself and God. If he even starts to lie, he now immediately admits it. Seeing such honesty, the wife developed a renewed trust in her husband. Both are now spiritually thriving, God has become the centerpiece in their home. With the counselor's sustained guidance and God's transforming power, they both are now closer to the examples that God designed them to be. With the tools in hand from the wise counselor, thoughts and feelings are now vetted and treated as what they truly are, thoughts and feelings. Not an issue has arisen in the last year that this couple could not resolve. Stability, peace, and love now reign in this wonderful home.

A closing note, this story was entirely constructed from an interview with the husband and wife, *not* the counselor. The counselor provides a place of confidentiality for those whom they provide advice. Christian counseling is a noble profession with tremendous capacity for performing good works.

The Safe Haven

A caring woman sacrificially left a job with better pay and benefits to work with teens at a high school. She believed God had placed her there but working with teens on a daily basis has its challenges. She felt the kids needed a safe haven, a place where they could come and feel accepted and confidentially share their problems. Her work area became that place. To create such an environment, she has tolerated being spat on, hit, cursed, and had water thrown on her. She does not hold it against the students, because she knows that they never were mad at her, but at school rules, parents, circumstances, or themselves. Knowing that she personally cares about them in a non-judgmental way, they will often listen to her advice. They recognize that she loves them and will always tell them the truth, not just something they want to hear. Through the years, she has developed some deep relationships with some of these teens or as she calls them "her kids." Through these relationships, bonds of trust grew, which allowed her to have a significant impact on some of the kids' lives.

On one occasion, she noticed one of the girls was frequently coming to school and getting sick in the morning. The girl confided with her that she had been having unprotected sex, so this caring woman gave the girl some money for a pregnancy test. Regrettably, it came back positive. The girl was hysterical. As the woman advised, she had the test confirmed at the local health department. Totally frantic, the young girl came to her caring confidant and shared her fears. Not only was her boyfriend going to be upset, but she felt her parents would be beyond upset and could throw her out of the house. The caring woman put forward some sound advice on how to approach her parents to help mitigate their reaction. So the fretting pregnant teen told her mother first. Her mom was initially upset but soon accepted the situation. Then they went to her father and told him together. The dad completely lost it. He was extremely shocked and angry with his daughter's careless behavior and immediately threw her against the wall. The distraught teen tearfully left her house. She stayed with someone else for a couple of nights to let her dad cool off before she returned home.

Another problem that resulted from her pregnancy would test the young girl to the core of her being. Her boyfriend demanded that she get an abortion. He said that he could not afford to support a child, so the course of action appeared to be simple to him. He told her that he would provide the money for the abortion. The conflicted girl returned to her safe haven since she had come to trust the advice of her wise confidant. She needed help thinking through what might be the most important decision she would ever make. After the young girl shared her boyfriend's take on the situation, the caring woman provided the following advice, "You have shared with me some of your dreams. You love children and look forward to having them. You might not be able to handle the psychological and spiritual aftermath of having an abortion. Guilt will likely overwhelm you and you will be sorry the rest of your life. You have told me that you believe that to abort a child is wrong, and it is. As for your boyfriend's desires, it is not about him at this point. Don't do anything before you thoroughly think this through and pray over it, and I will pray for God to guide your decision."

Sadly, her boyfriend broke up with her because she decided to keep the baby. The caring confidant knew she would need to help the inexperienced teen through the coming days. She first bought her a book titled *What to Expect When You're Expecting* to help her understand the changes she would experience throughout her pregnancy. They also discussed the travails that having a baby would bring as she tried to complete high school. Unfortunately, the young girl started experiencing a severe case of morning sickness and vomited violently every day for weeks. The caring woman again came to the rescue and bought her some ginger tablets to help relieve the morning sickness, but the problem was totally relieved when she acquired some ginger root and brewed the girl some tea. She taught the girl's mother how to do this, and it worked well.

The young girl's pregnancy started to wear her out. It was difficult to see her friends having fun, and she was tempted to quit school. But she was a good student and hung in there with the support of the caring woman. Before graduating, she delivered a baby boy. Her caring confidant continued to impact her life, as she bought the girl a breast pump which she could not afford. This enabled her mother and grandmother to care for her son as she finished high school. She also went home to nurse the baby at lunch. The caring woman bought the little one some clothes and helped with the baby shower. Life became a blessing for the young mother. She loves her baby. She loves being a mother. She found the man of her dreams and got married. She shared the following with her confidant; "You told me that it would all be worth it, and it really is. Life is not about me anymore but about him, my precious son."

God obviously was at work. He knew the caring woman's gifts of nurturing and accepting others would serve her well at the high school. Her unrelenting determination to help "her kids" work through their problems and pray for their needs demonstrates her love for them. As you just read, a precious life was saved, and that was not the only one. Yes, God placed this caring woman in that high school for such times as these.

Questions

1. What concerns exist when we decide to pursue vengeance? Describe how internally things might escalate.

2. Why is it important to let God administer vengeance?

3. After being hurt by someone, how do we overcome this evil? Describe this specifically with an example.

4. How might we fall short in pursuing peace with someone who has hurt us even though we did not do anything vengeful in response? What might be the ultimate ramifications of falling short in such cases?

5. In the story of Abigail and David, describe how Abigail overcame David's rage with a good deed?

6. Have you ever (or have you ever seen someone) overcome evil with good that involved not only forgiveness but performing good deeds? What do you think was the key to eventually bringing peace to the situation (assuming that was the case)? If you have never experienced (or seen) evil overcome by good, why do you think that is the case?

7. What do you think are the most important Christian attributes that will aid us spiritually in overcoming evil with good?

CHAPTER 8

Moving Forward

Search me, O God and know my heart;
Try me and know my anxious thoughts;
And see if there be any hurtful way in me,
And lead me in the everlasting way.

(Ps. 139:23-24)

A couple months after I started working for NASA, the first Space Shuttle Orbiter, the *Columbia*, was delivered to the Kennedy Space Center (KSC). She was in various stages of assembly and still required quite a bit of work. I remember the excitement and energy in the workforce at the time. *Columbia* was destined for space, and we had the privilege of preparing her for her maiden voyage. Since I had just graduated from college, most of my early assignments were fairly simple and mundane. Even though they hired me as a "rocket scientist," quite a bit of training and mentoring would have to occur before that label truly fit, and I could be given some of the more serious assignments. Nevertheless, I yearned to perform those important tasks, so patience and perseverance became two valuable qualities for me at that stage of my career.

A little over a year after the delivery of the *Columbia*, we were preparing a major integrated test that would exercise as many systems together as possible. The test involved performing countdowns and ascent runs that included many of the abort scenarios. Simulated sensor data was substituted for the flight data, where required, to make the flight computers deduce that the *Columbia* was actually going through a real launch countdown, liftoff, and ascent profile. To verify that all the facets of this highly involved test were properly working together, we went to the Shuttle Avionics Integration Laboratory at the Johnson Space Center to perform each of the mission runs until we were confident the integrated test would succeed at KSC. We had two crews of people working around the clock for three weeks straight to get everything in working order. This was a grueling and complex project.

The work was exhausting, but for me personally, a particular event occurred that set my career on a new trajectory. During one of the mission runs, two of the Space Shuttle Main Engines (SSME) did not start (simulated) as expected. Almost everyone believed that the equipment, which was designed to simulate the SSMEs was to blame, but I was not convinced that this was the problem. I spent much time and effort evaluating a great deal of information and became convinced that the start commands had never been issued by the actual flight computers. When I took the problem to our IBM experts, they doubted my conclusions but soon discovered that the priority for the commands to be sent to the engines was set too low in the flight software. With all of the extra computing activity required to process the simulated data, the flight computers were not always completing their tasks; so, on occasion, they would fail to send one or more of the start commands to the engines.

I share this story, not to stroke my ego, but to demonstrate how my involvement with this problem broke down some of the barriers of youth and inexperience I faced early in my career. Afterward, I started receiving more important assignments. I was asked to attend meetings to which in the past I would not have been invited. People started paying attention to my opinions and called me in on certain problems. I guess I was beginning to earn the status as "certified rocket scientist" (just kidding, of course).

Paul's missionary partner, Timothy, was also acquainted with the barriers of youth. Paul told the young enthusiast for the gospel the following:

> Prescribe and teach these things. Let no one look down on your youthfulness, but *rather* in speech, conduct, love, faith *and* purity, show yourself an example of those who believe (1 Tim. 4:11-12).

Even this devoted evangelist was not immune to the barriers

that youthfulness might put in his path. Paul shared with the young man that the best way to win over the hearts of those to whom he ministered was to live and walk the transformed life of a true Christian. This would provide them proof of his spiritual maturity and help tear down a barrier of youth.

When it comes to performing good deeds, most of us have some barriers to break down as well. These barriers can be quite diverse and may be real or perceived and involve such things as spirituality, age, abilities, confidence, fears, biases, appearance, physical limitations, illness, geography, financial circumstances, culture, politics, legalities, religion, trust, faith, comfort levels, personal preferences, education/training, and incorrect perceptions/thinking. I am sure you could add to this list, but hopefully you get the gist. Since some barriers may stand in our way of fulfilling our divinely given purpose of engaging in good works, we might need to address some of them prior to moving forward in our service to God. Of course, some of these barriers are beyond our control, and we cannot let them detract us from going after what we can control. Obviously, it is well beyond the scope of this book to try to tackle all these barriers, nevertheless within its chapters you can find some valuable suggestions concerning some of them. Let's look at the following story to see some of the particular barriers a woman in Jesus' time had to overcome to perform a good deed for Him.

Breaching Treacherous Walls

Simon the Pharisee was undoubtedly intrigued by Jesus, so he invited Him to dinner to find out for himself what all the fuss was about concerning Him. During a meal involving someone of notoriety like Jesus, Simon may have left the door open per the custom of the day to allow others to come in and sit along the walls to listen to the conversation.[31] A woman who was desperate to show her love for Jesus shockingly broke down multiple barriers at the dinner to make it happen.

Now one of the Pharisees was requesting Him to dine with him, and He entered the Pharisee's house and reclined *at the table*. And there was a woman in the city who was a sinner; and when she learned that He was reclining *at the table* in the Pharisee's house, she brought an alabaster vial of perfume, and standing behind *Him* at His feet, weeping, she began to wet His feet with her tears, and kept wiping them with the hair of her head, and kissing His feet and anointing them with the perfume. Now when the Pharisee who had invited Him saw this, he said to himself, "If this man were a prophet He would know who and what sort of person this woman is who is touching Him, that she is a sinner." And Jesus answered and said to him, "Simon, I have something to say to you." And he replied, "Say it, Teacher." "A moneylender had two debtors: one owed five hundred denarii, and the other fifty. When they were unable to repay, he graciously forgave them both. Which of them will love him more?" Simon answered and said, "I suppose the one whom he forgave more." And He said to him, "You have judged correctly." And turning toward the woman, He said to Simon, "Do you see this woman? I entered your house; you gave Me no water for My feet, but she has wet My feet with her tears, and wiped them with her hair. You gave Me no kiss; but she, since the time I came in, has not ceased to kiss My feet. You did not anoint My head with oil, but she anointed My feet with perfume. For this reason I say to you, her sins, which are many, have been forgiven, for she loved much; but he who is forgiven little, loves little." Then He said to her, "Your sins have been forgiven." Those who were reclining *at the table* with Him began to say to themselves, "Who is this *man* who even forgives sins?" And He said to the woman, "Your faith has saved you; go in peace" (Lk. 7:36-50).

To properly understand this story, I want to make sure you recognize some of its features. Luke identified the woman as a "sinner" (v. 37). In all likelihood, this involved some sort of sexual immorality, perhaps prostitution. Simon's thoughts concerning her seemed to imply this, but the text falls short in allowing us to make a definite decision. Another important aspect of the story involved the woman's forgiveness. Jesus used the parable to show Simon that if someone had been forgiven much, they would correspondingly love much. Thus, the woman's loving gratitude was in response to forgiveness she had already received. Perhaps this occurred in a previous encounter with Jesus or due to being baptized by John the Baptist (ref. Lk. 3:3). Luke does not provide us with these details, but interestingly, this story was placed immediately after a discussion involving John the Baptist. In fact in verses 29 and 30, Luke referred to "all the people" who had been baptized by John and noted that the Pharisees had not. We can see then why Jesus might have contrasted Simon's behavior with the woman's. Jesus divinely validated to both Simon and the woman that her sins had been forgiven. He then succinctly stated that her faith "saved" her (v. 50), not her love. Again, her incredible expression of love was in response to an incredible amount of forgiveness. Whether you agree with my interpretation or prefer another, it is important to realize that the barriers that the woman had to overcome would be the same.

Please accept the following as a possible reconstruction of what happened around Simon's dinner table to help us better understand the story. As the woman left the safety of the outskirts of the room, she paused at Jesus' feet. She wanted to anoint His head but had no access to it because of the dinner guest reclining next to Him. An unexpected release of emotions started to come over her. Fueled by a perplexing mixture of past regrets and gratefulness for her newfound peace, tears started to roll down her cheeks and accidentally drop onto Jesus' feet. Since she initially intended to anoint His head, she had no towel to wipe up the tears. After kneeling, she let down her long-flowing hair and used it to tenderly wipe Jesus' tear-moistened feet. With this unexpected turn in events, she changed her strategy for the perfume and broke the bottle at its long neck and poured the fragrant fluid on his feet. An impassioned gratitude rushed over her and she started to kiss his feet.[32]

Now let's look at the specific barriers this woman faced to accomplish this good deed for Jesus.

- As a woman, to approach Jesus in such a way went against the norms of this culture.

- In any culture, such an act would require one to overcome various fears.

- The woman was also publicly known as a "sinner" and would have to face potential humiliation.

- Many individuals would quickly leave the room to avoid crying in front of others.

- Letting her hair down in public was a shameful practice.[33]

- Approaching Jesus put her at risk of being rejected by Him.[34] Not that He would, but she could not know that.

- Luke probably mentioned that the perfume was contained in an "alabaster vial" to denote its value. The expense of using a hand-carved alabaster vial was justified because of the precious ointments and perfumes they contained.[35] Undoubtedly, this woman financially sacrificed by breaking open this costly bottle of perfume and using it on Jesus. To her, Jesus was worth the cost. We must ask ourselves as well, "Is Jesus worth the cost?"

Please note that Jesus does not stop this expression of love. If you were sitting by the wall would you have tried to restrain her? If you were Simon, would you ask her to leave your house? Jesus understood what was transpiring. That was the way forgiven people were supposed to respond, so why stop her. Also, Simon needed to learn from this "sinner." Simon showed Jesus no affection, while the woman's love toward Him was extravagant yet humble. Do you have anything to learn from this "sinner"?

Your Barriers

For many good deeds, we just need to start doing them. Nothing is complicated or scary about them; we just need to apply ourselves and get to work. Maybe your barriers are minimal, and you simply need to fine tune a few things before getting started. After performing a good deed or two, some of you may wonder why you ever had any apprehensions in the first place. You might have needed a little push, and this book (or something else) has accomplished that for you. Hopefully, performing good works will become second nature to you, allowing you to easily see and act on the opportunities that God has set before you.

What if you passionately desire to address an area of specific needs that cause others to struggle in life, but you are encountering some anxieties that are holding you back. What should you do? First, try to identify what potential barriers may be standing in your way. You may need a trusted confidant to help you compile this list, as some barriers might be subtle or unconscious and require some gentle prodding by your confidant to surface them. Secondly, once you have formulated your list, you might be able to address some of the barriers yourself, but you may need to seek advice from someone experienced in these concerns. For example, before you try to help someone overcome a spiritual issue, you may need to go to a minister to identify and clarify some specific passages that deal with the specific area of concern. Never be afraid to admit that you may not be ready to perform a specific good work. Just make sure that you do not strand somebody who is in desperate need; try to find someone who can help them. Also, some barriers may require you to make a short-range or long-range plan to remove or mitigate the barrier. For instance, you might go to a counselor to help you come up with a plan to deal with your lack of confidence or to address a particular fear. Let's look at a few examples of breaking down some specific barriers.

All of us have fears, and we likely won't need to address most of them with a counselor. As you well know, those first-time jitters just need a dose or two of getting to work, and they typically will go away. For many good deeds, our fears will leave us as we receive the proper training, education, or mentoring. And as you continue to reach out to others, your confidence will grow, and your fears will typically subside. However, it is hard to predict how we will react in all situations, so that is why courage is important as we face our fears head-on. You might also want to review the discussion about courage in chapter four.

One remarkable woman shared with me how she brought her family together to discuss a situation with unknown and potentially risky outcomes to help her rise above her fears. She and her husband were attending their church's worship service one Sunday morning and during the announcements a peculiar request was made. The youth minister and his wife had planned on adopting a particular baby in a few weeks. Due to an emergency situation, they were called on to adopt another infant, so the youth minister was pleading with his congregation for someone to step forward and adopt the baby that was originally destined for him and his wife. The remarkable woman's husband said, "I think we can do this" and suggested that they go home and pray about it. However, the wife had some serious reservations. Raising another child did not concern her, as they already had five children. Her apprehension was that the child was of another race. It was not a matter of discrimination. It was the fear of the unknown. She found herself wrestling with several questions. How would others treat her children? How would the child fit in? How would their friends react? Could they financially afford the expenses associated with a private adoption? To overcome these fears, the entire family discussed their concerns and prayed about them together. They committed collectively to fully embrace this baby as part of their family. The situation worked out well through the years. The girl turned out to be a happy, confident, and content young lady. Their church and friends showered them with gifts and eased the family's financial burden. The remarkable woman said, "God always provides a way." By the way, this remarkable woman kept God pretty busy as they went on to adopt three more children and fostered sixty-eight (many being special needs children). Now you see why she was "remarkable."

Sometimes the good works God sets before us may require a significant investment of time and resources on our part. When I started down the path on which I currently am, I quickly recognized I needed to acquire the proper education and training to give me the credentials, capabilities, and knowledge needed to write Christian literature and to speak publicly. I found that even though I started to address these barriers, it would take me a number of years to complete my degree program. I wish that I could have accomplished it sooner, but I also had committed to be a Christian husband and parent. Parenting two teens came with a lot of challenges, and I needed to perform a lot of good works in their lives to prepare them for a precarious world. Be patient with overcoming the barriers you face and make certain that you are properly prepared before you begin to address specific needs. I am not trying to introduce any doubts in your mind. I just want you to use good judgment so that you are rightly prepared for your chosen good works. But please, when you are ready, act! It is a personally rewarding aspect of my work today to bring spiritual richness and the goodness of God to others through my writings and talks.

Paul dealt with a number of barriers while ministering to the Corinthian church. He did not dazzle them with wise speech like the other Greek philosophers of his day. His appearance and meager existence appeared counter to his claim to be an apostle. He had a physical weakness that seemed contrary to someone God had supposedly blessed. They even wondered why he had not presented them with letters of commendation. Paul counteracted these barriers with several things. His understanding of Scripture and the grace of God was phenomenal. His teachings were sound. His example was pure and exemplary. And because of this, the Corinthians could unmistakably see the result of his works in their lives. Their hearts revealed the evidence of Paul's ministry and consequently were his letters of commendation; penned by the "Spirit of the living God" (2 Cor. 3:3). Because of his weakness, the results they exhibited in their own lives were ample evidence that God was working through him, because He could not accomplish such results otherwise. Trusting God, imitating Christ, living the transformed life, teaching the gospel in its purity, and past preparation led to Paul's successful ministry.

Let's identify those barriers, address them the best you can, and perform those good works God has prepared for you to accomplish.

■ YOUR GOOD DEED TO PONDER

The last good deed to ponder is your own. You have read about a variety of good works. You became acquainted with the passions of those who reached out to others in need. You saw how their gifts were utilized to accomplish their gracious actions. You could see the evidence of God at work in their lives. Has your heart been touched by these stories? Have they sparked a flame of passion in you to address a specific need in the lives of others? Have you discovered new venues where you can apply your gifts for God? You know the tasks for which God's workmanship has prepared you; are you ready to engage in good deeds?

I would like for you to create your own "Good Deeds to Ponder" story. Put together a fictitious situation in which someone has a pressing need (make sure this is a need that you are personally interested in helping others address), along with the specific good work you performed to help them. Include how you became aware of their need. Integrate into the story the importance of your zeal and how you went about approaching others to perform the good deed. Include how your specific God-given gifts were utilized and what you hoped to accomplish in the life of the one(s) to whom you reached out. Note how God was providentially working in and through you to address the pressing need. Please address any barriers you needed to overcome and how you eliminated them. Obviously, this is a work of fiction, but it entails who you want to become. God can help you make it a reality.

Lastly, I hope you will continue to mull over the many challenging aspects of this book that you have taken your precious time to read. Good deeds come in many forms and may this work of passion continue to speak to your heart and stimulate you to take the goodness of God into the lives of others.

Questions

1. What barriers, anxieties, or apprehensions stand in your way of accomplishing your divinely given purpose of engaging in good deeds? How might you address each of them?

2. Have you discovered a pressing need that others face in their lives that you would like to help address? What do you need to do to start down this path?

3. Have you discovered how any of your gifts, talents, or skills might assist you in serving others in a new way? Describe how you might use them in this new manner?

4. What was the most important thing you learned in reading this book?

5. Did you write your "Good Deeds to Ponder" story? If you are uncomfortable writing it, please list the highlights that might make up such a story.

Endnotes

Chapter 1

1 Unless otherwise noted, all biblical references in this book are taken from *New American Standard Bible*. 1995.

2 M. Robert Mulholland, *Invitation to a Journey: A Road Map for Spiritual Formation* (Downers Grove, IL: InterVarsity Press, 1993), p. 43-44.

3 Richard R. Melick, *Philippians Colossians Philemon*, The New American Commentary, vol. 32, (Nashville, TN: Broadman & Holman Publishers, 1991), 58-59.

4 Albert T. Lincoln, *Ephesians*, Word Biblical Commentary, vol. 42 (Dallas, TX: Word Books, 1990), 116.

Chapter 2

5 William M. Golden, "A Beautiful Life," words by William M. Golden.

6 D. A. Carson, *Matthew*, The Expositor's Bible Commentary, vol. 8, (Grand Rapids: Zondervan, 1984), 139.

7 Richard Nelson, *First and Second Kings*, Interpretation, (Louisville: John Knox Press, 1987), 173.

8 Gwilym H. Jones, *I and II Kings*, The New Century Bible Commentary, (Grand Rapids, MI: Eerdmans, 1984), 405.

Chapter 3

9 Gordon D. Fee, *1 and 2 Timothy, Titus*, New International Biblical Commentary, (Peabody, MA: Hendrickson Publishers, 1988), 180.

10 Philip H. Towner, *1-2 Timothy & Titus*, The IVP New Testament Commentary Series, (Downers Grove, IL: InterVarsity Press, 1994), 230.

11 William D. Mounce, *Pastoral Epistles*, Word Biblical Commentary, vol. 46, (Nashville, TN: Thomas Nelson, 2000), 432.

12 Jeanie Lerche Davis, "The Science of Good Deeds: The 'helper's high' could help you live a longer, healthier life," *WebMD.com* (2005) [on-line article]; available from http://www.webmd.com/balance/features/science-good-deeds; accessed 19 May 2015.

"Why Giving is Good for Your Health," *ClevelandClinic.org*, (2 Dec. 2014); [on-line article]; available from http://health.clevelandclinic.org/2014/12/why-giving-is-good-for-your-health/; accessed 19 May 2015.

Allen Luks, *The Healing Power of Doing Good: The Health and Spiritual Benefits of Helping Others* (New York: Fawcett Columbine, 1991), 17.

Chapter 4

13 Craig S. Keener, *Matthew*, The IVP New Testament Commentary Series, (Downers Grove, IL: InterVarsity Press, 1997), 169-70.

14 Craig A. Evans, *Mark 8:27-16:20*, Word Biblical Commentary, (Nashville, TN: Thomas Nelson Publishers, 2001), 518-19.

15 David John Ford, *Confessions of a Small Town Minister* (Bloomington, IN: Westbow Press, 2014), 110.

16 Carson, *Matthew*, 520.

17 Robert H. Stein, *Luke*, The New American Commentary, vol. 24, (Nashville, TN: Broadman Press, 1992), 317.

Chapter 5

18 Walter Bauer, *A Greek-English Lexicon of the New Testament and other Early Christian Literature*, 3rd ed., rev. Frederick William Danker (Chicago: University of Chicago Press, 2000), 870 &1066.

19 Ronald Y. K. Fung, *The Epistle to the Galatians*, The New International Commentary on the New Testament, (Grand Rapids, MI: Eerdmans, 1988), 268.

20 Darrell L. Bock, Acts, Baker Exegetical Commentary on the New Testament, (Grand Rapids, MI: Baker Academic, 2007), 377.

21 F. F. Bruce believes the middle voice of the Greek grammar suggests that the widows were wearing the garments they showed Peter. F. F. Bruce, *Commentary on the Book of Acts*, The New International Commentary on the New Testament, (Grand Rapids, MI: Eerdmans, 1977), 212.

Chapter 6

22 Charles R. Swindoll, *Improving Your Serve: The Art of Unselfish Living* (Waco, TX: Word Books, 1981), 163.

23 D.A. Carson, *The Gospel According to John*, The Pillar New Testament Commentary, (Grand Rapids, MI: Eerdmans, 1991), 169-70.

24 Mark Mangano, *Esther & Daniel*, The College Press NIV Commentary, (Joplin, MO: College Press, 2001).

Chapter 7

25 Much of this paragraph was derived from a couple paragraphs in my first book. Michael O'Neal, *An Angel's View: Encountering God through the Stories of the Heavenly Hosts* (Nashville, TN: 21st Century Christian, 2010), 166-67.

26 Carson, *Matthew*, 156.

27 Jack Cottrell, *Romans Volume 2*, The College Press NIV Commentary, (Joplin, MO: College Press, 1998), 346-47.

28 Ibid., 352-53.

29 Robert D. Bergen, *1, 2 Samuel*, The New American Commentary, vol. 7, (Nashville, TN: Broadman & Holman Publishers, 2002), 245-46.

30 Ibid, 247.

Chapter 8

31 Darrell L. Bock, *Luke*, The NIV Application Commentary, (Grand Rapids, MI: Zondervan, 1996), 218.

32 John Nolland, *Luke* 1-9:20, Word Bible Commentary, vol. 35A, (Dallas, TX: Word Books, 1989), 354.

33 Stein, *Luke*, 236.

34 Bock, *Luke*, 224.

35 Nolland, *Luke*, 354.

CPSIA information can be obtained
at www.ICGtesting.com
Printed in the USA
BVHW081542050121
596840BV00008B/601